P9-CMF-839

DISCARDED

DISCARDED

PRODUCING SCHOOL PLAYS

PRODUCING SCHOOL PLAYS

[Photo by Author.

R.U.R., Epilogue. "Look, Helena! The Dawn is breaking."
A school production with an all-boy cast.

PRODUCING SCHOOL PLAYS

BY

ERNEST F. DYER, B.A. (Lond.)

ENGLISH MASTER, HEATON SECONDARY SCHOOL FOR BOYS
NEWCASTLE-UPON-TYNE

Lenoir Rhyne College
LIBRARY

THOMAS NELSON AND SONS, Ltd.
LONDON, EDINBURGH, NEW YORK
TORONTO, AND PARIS

CONTENTS

6　　　　　　　　Contents

Note on Plates.—Except where separate acknowledgment is made, the reproductions from photographs relate to productions at Heaton Secondary Boys' School, Newcastle-upon-Tyne.

AUTHOR'S NOTE

THIS book is the outcome of adventures in dramatic work at Heaton Secondary School, Newcastle-upon-Tyne. We began, some six or seven years ago, knowing precariously little about the practical points of the game. We had a splendid new hall, but no proper stage, and no equipment whatever. We blundered blindly along for a time, and then we began to look around to see what we could learn from established theatric technique and from experiments on the contemporary stage. We are still learning ; but in the meantime we have acquired a certain confidence in ourselves—we feel more sure of our aims and methods, and not a little proud of our equipment. We think that if we were compelled by flood, fire, or earthquake, to start all over again, we should make a more efficient and economical job of it the second time. The book, therefore, may conceivably help other schools to profit from our initial mistakes, for though books on production are now far more plentiful than they were two or three years ago there still seems to be nothing else tackling the problem directly from the school angle, though the admirable work by Jeffreys and Stopford, published after the bulk of this book was written, comes fairly near.

Glancing through the chapters which follow I am left with one grievous apprehension—that I have failed to convey the glorious fun of it all. The production of a play, it is true, has definite artistic implications ; it calls for study, time, patience, and hard work ; it needs to be sustained by " an enthusiasm allied to madness." But it is such fun.

Much of the material contained in the book first appeared in the columns of *The Schoolmaster* during the summer of 1931, and I have to thank the editor of that journal for allowing me to use it here. It has, however, been thoroughly revised in the light of experience.

I wish also to thank those who have helped me in the preparation of this book : my colleague, Mr. H. Bambrough, for writing the appendix on the switchboard ; Mr. John Hampden for writing Appendices I., IV., and V., and for many incidental favours ; Mr. M. V. C. Jeffreys, of the Institute of Education, for allowing me to reproduce the drawings of his model stage, and for much helpful encouragement ; my headmaster, Mr. F. R. Barnes, for his generous help and advice ; my colleague, Mr. J. A. Waldron, who has borne the brunt of the practical work of our productions, for his invaluable co-operation ; Paul Jeffreys and Bert Brown for assistance in the preparation of certain diagrams ; and the following for permission to use photographs : Lee Simonson, of New York City ; Miss Gertrude Ingham, Principal of Moira House School, Eastbourne, and the Vice-Principal and Producer, Miss Mona Swann ; Mr. Mordaunt Shairp, of University College School, Hampstead ; Mr. A. K. Boyd, of Radley College, Bucks.   E. F. D.

They make all their scholars play-boys ! Is't not a fine sight, to see all our children made interluders ? Do we pay our money for this ? We send them to learn their grammar and their Terence, and they learn their play-books !—BEN JONSON, *The Staple of News.*

We know that drama, like music, lives in performance alone.—ASHLEY DUKES, *The World to Play With.*

The Art of the Theatre is neither acting nor the play, it is not scene nor dance, but it consists of all the elements of which these things are composed : action, which is the very spirit of acting ; words, which are the body of the play ; line and colour, which are the very heart of scene ; rhythm, which is the very essence of dance.
GORDON CRAIG, *On the Art of the Theatre.*

PRODUCING SCHOOL PLAYS

CHAPTER I.—THE PLAY AND THE PRODUCER

1. The Meaning of Play Production

THE place of drama in the schools is now established. The methods of Mr. Caldwell Cook and others like him have swept " like a healthful breeze " through the English classrooms of the country. The play-way has become the everyday way.

The enthusiasm of the classroom, naturally enough, has overflowed. Informal " end of term shows " and " rags " there always have been, and, let us hope, always will be, but now we find form plays and house plays coming to stand alongside games and athletics as symbols of group endeavour. And, while this has been happening inside the school community, the performances given by schools before the general public have undergone a corresponding development. Only a few years ago schools contented themselves with dramatic interludes—for the most part glorified recitations—introduced, with much official misgiving, to enliven the somewhat drouthy proceedings of Speech Days ; now the vast majority of schools undertake regular dramatic performances, increasingly ambitious in scope, appealing to audiences extending far beyond the mere relatives of the performers, and often possessing genuine artistic validity.

Such public performances, of course, are not entirely modern. As long ago as 1527 and 1528 we hear of the boys of

St. Paul's School acting in elaborately staged plays before
audiences which included the king and Wolsey ; other schools
of that time accepted the acting of plays as a method of educational training, and helped to nourish the art which flowered
at the close of Elizabeth's reign.   It may be that the schools of
to-day have a similar contribution to make to the enrichment
of the national life.

The development of public performances has necessarily
imposed heavy duties and responsibilities on certain teachers
in the schools, duties and responsibilities which most of them
have welcomed, but for which, in many cases, they have been
unequipped and unprepared.   They have had to learn the
job of " producing " for themselves, by the hard and often
wasteful process of trial and error.   It is such teachers that
this book is designed primarily to assist.

The chapters which follow, therefore, while they will
include hints on stage technique and rehearsal method, many
of which should be equally applicable to work inside the
classroom, will contain suggestions upon such practical matters
as the simple equipment of stages, the making of settings, the
choice and construction of lighting units.

The extension of play performance from the classroom to
the stage has been largely accidental and unpremeditated.
The motive perhaps has been rather to exhibit than to enter-
tain.   Schools have seldom thought out the full artistic implications of the task to which they were setting their hand.
Caldwell Cook himself was not concerned to train actors,
but to allow boys to indulge their play-acting instinct—an
admirable but a different thing.   It is one thing to act plays
in a form-room ; immediately they are presented upon a stage
before an audience a new set of conditions is established.
When a play is staged, a new entity, a new work of art, is born.
Acting is but one element in it, speech another ; lighting,
scene, movement—all make their various appeals to the mind

of the spectator. The play becomes the sum of these appeals ; the aim of production is their perfect co-ordination to make the drama live for the audience " at its highest possible emotional intensity." [1]

It is fatal, therefore, to regard play production as a mere extension of the English lesson. We have in this matter, if we are sincere about it, to break away from the " literary tradition," which is as big a menace to drama as the stage tradition is to the essentially different art of cinema. (If people, says St. John Ervine, " will cease to regard Shakespeare as a literary gent, and will begin to think of him as a man of the theatre, they will come much nearer to a proper appreciation of his plays." [2]) The art of words is one thing ; the art of the theatre is another. Each has its mysteries. Let us not be guilty of confusing them.

Whether the educational value of the more ambitious order of public performance is worth the time spent on their preparation will depend upon both the quality of the play and the quality of the production. The question cannot be given a categorical answer. But it is the writer's conviction that there is a value to the individual gained from the careful and constant rehearsal of a play for performance that is different in its character from the value to be derived from dramatic work as part of the English lesson in the classroom, and that this value becomes greater as the various contributory arts of production, such as motion, scene, lighting, are employed.

All this talk of " contributory arts " may sound very terrifying to schools which have to equip their stages from the barest resources. But it is the use to which equipment is put, not its cost, which is the issue. The finest effects may be achieved with the simplest of means. The only lavishness

---

[1] Selden.

[2] *Cp.* W. A. Darlington in his *Life of Sheridan* : " Plays are not, in fact, literary compositions at all, and any merit they may happen to have as reading matter is incidental, if not accidental."

which is necessary is that instanced recently by Ivor Brown when, praising the simplicity of a production, he wrote, " No brains had been spared." It is almost pathetic to find schools (as one can) dissipating such resources as they have upon elaborate (and out-moded) scenery for occasional productions instead of building up a stock of general " all-purposes " stage equipment which can be put to continual use.[1] This book, in dealing with equipment, will try to emphasize the purpose it is intended to serve.

What that purpose is, of course, depends upon one's conception of what stage presentation ought to be—and on that subject the last thirty years have witnessed a revolution in idea. For the most part the movement has been one of simplification and of reliance upon the formal and the abstract, rather than upon the realistic, as affording the most adequate and appropriate background to theatric action. School producers, who are inevitably working with simple means, can learn far more from this movement than by attempting feeble imitations of what they see in the conventional commercial theatre where " stage decoration " is still, for the most part, synonymous with painting scenery. Incidentally, they may be helping to educate the public mind to appreciate what is really vital and essential in drama.

Our job is to make our performances artistically sincere and theatrically intelligent—and on a minimum of expense. The place of the drama in the schools is already established : let us establish in them the art of the theatre.

2. The Nature of the Performance

Variety and versatility in dramatic enterprise in the school should be encouraged. It would be tragic if emphasis on the

[1] See page 151.

more ambitious form of school entertainment were to weaken
the springs of simple, spontaneous endeavour. In the writer's
experience the danger is not serious : he finds that the more
demands there are made upon the dramatic society by its
major production, the more original work and experiment there
is forthcoming in the school. This activity includes play-
readings by dramatic society groups, performances by house
or form groups of one-act plays or dramatized ballads on social
evenings, or before an audience of the whole school on the last
afternoon of term, and the work of the Stage-craft Guild which
is described in Chapter X. An interesting and inspiring
account of dramatic activity in a Surrey school is contributed by Mr. John Hampden in Appendix I.

As for public " shows," it is the practice in the writer's
school for the annual performances of play or opera to be
given (usually for three or four nights) towards the end of the
spring term ; this production is as carefully prepared and as
highly polished as possible. A week or two later one or two
invitation performances are given of a miscellaneous entertainment, the programme for which usually includes burlesques
of the society's efforts in its main production, one-act plays
chosen from those performed by groups during the season (and,
perhaps, produced by the boys themselves), performances of
ballads, dancing, and musical items, and others such as are
hinted at in Chapter XI.

The keynote of this " Revue " is high spirits ; nothing
likely to offend artistic good manners is tolerated, the standard
of taste demanded in staging and lighting is high, and genuine
theatric beauty is as likely to be attained (though perhaps not
sustained) on this occasion as upon the more formal.

Such experience as he has had with this kind of performance
inclines the writer to agree with the dramatic critic of the
Manchester Guardian, who, describing " an original and ad-
venturous programme " (at the Manchester High School),

consisting of short plays, sketches, and "a miniature panto-mime," suggested that "such a piece, in which dancing and pageantry play a large part, is much more suitable for young players than the difficult scenes from Shakespeare which used to be the standard subjects of school performances." [1]

In the selection of a full-length play some governing considerations may be suggested :

1. It should be a play intrinsically worth doing—the energies of a school are not well spent in producing pleasant rubbish which can be done much more competently by a professional touring company.

2. It should make demands on the audience as well as on the players—it should be a contribution to the cultural life of the district. (Jones Major defines a school as "an institution to help children educate their parents.")

3. It should provide opportunities for a large number of players and stage assistants—this, it must be confessed, has a box-office as well as an educational value.

4. It should be a play which appeals to the producer—he cannot do justice to a work he does not appreciate.

5. It should be the *type* of play that is within the scope of the company.

No. 5 demands some elaboration.

(*a*) It should not demand scenic or lighting effects which cannot be provided.

(*b*) It should not depend—like so many West End successes attempted by misguided amateurs—upon a slick acting technique which the players do not possess.

(*c*) It should not demand speaking qualities which are not inherent in the cast ; verse plays, for example, should not be chosen unless there is a reasonable prospect of having them

---

[1] The question is not the educational value of acting Shakespeare ; that is beyond dispute. It is whether the exhibition of these educational exercises is suitable public entertainment. But it is chiefly against the *exclusive* performance of Shakespeare by schools that I would enter a mild protest."—E. F. D.

adequately spoken ; Cockney speakers should avoid modern
plays of high society life.

[It is difficult to decide upon the importance of dialectal
elements in speech. When the writer first went to teach in
the north of England the accents of his pupils so jarred upon
his sensibilities (as doubtless did his southern noises upon
theirs—and as either set of sounds would have jarred upon
Shakespeare's) that the idea of their performing, say, *The
Tempest*, seemed to him little short of blasphemous. Now, of
course, after a number of years he finds his ears sufficiently
attuned to local sounds to discount them. As long as verse is
well enunciated he can enjoy it. It would seem, then, that as
long as the audience is composed of people accustomed to hear
(and perhaps to use) the local accent, its employment will not
mar a play. People are more conscious of other dialects than
their own. (A part was played in a school play in the North
by a boy who hailed from the Midlands. His speech, though
not perfect, was nearer to the received standard than that of
the other players, yet he was the only player whose " accent "
excited comment in the audience.)

Upon occasion, frank use of local dialect should be made.
Traditional Cockney small parts, for instance, can often be
transposed, though the transposition will involve more than
a change in pronunciation ; each dialect has its distinctive
idiom and manner of phrasing. For this reason genuine
dialect plays (*e.g.* of Eden Philpotts or Ernest Bryan) must
be left to natives. If such plays exist in the local dialect,
use should be made of them. It will be found that boys
whose local accent is the broadest are by no means the best
speakers of genuine local dialect ; the " bi-lingualists " are
often better. Speaking in a dialect play actually helps to
improve a boy's accent, because it makes him more conscious
of speech differences.]

The school producer has one great advantage over the

Amateur Dramatic Society producer. The latter, working with adults who are for the most part already " set " in their acting methods, is forced to choose his play with the cast in mind. The school producer—unless, of course, his colleagues are participating—can afford to take a bigger risk. Obviously he would not select *Hamlet* or *Macbeth* unless he had some particular (and, in those cases, altogether exceptional) boy actor in mind; but for a multitude of parts he can bank on " discovering " in the school, if it be of normal size, the performers he requires. He is therefore free, within limits, to choose plays for their intrinsic suitability.

If the right choice of material is made, the enterprise will mean an enrichment of experience for the players, an enrichment of the cultural life of the locality, and a deepening of the corporate life of the school.

3. *The Producer*

" What the producer needs to know about the stage amounts exactly to everything there is to know."—C. B. PURDOM.

The Duties of a Producer.—In the first place, let us try to set down the main duties which fall to the school producer.

The responsibility of *choosing a play* he will perhaps share with a committee.

If his colleagues are taking part in the performance, he may be wise to share the responsibility of *casting* as well ; normally it should be his alone.

He is directly responsible for the *conduct and organization of rehearsals*. The conduct of rehearsals is the subject of Chapter II. The organization of them implies (*a*) covering all the ground in time ; (*b*) arranging them to suit people's leisure —doubly difficult when staff participate. He will ascertain

(3,982)

the previous engagements of his cast, and then prepare a weekly or fortnightly call-sheet.[1] (It will be noticed in the specimen that rehearsals are called for the lunch hour. We have found this to be so much the most convenient time, that when an opera involving many members of the staff is being rehearsed it is our practice to start afternoon school half an hour later on two days a week to allow adequate time.)

He is responsible for the *stage settings—the scenery, properties, and costumes*—and for every tint of colour used in the painting or making of them. (If he calls upon another person to design the settings—which is *not* advisable—the producer must explain to him exactly what he wants the designs to convey, and must be prepared to make from them the necessary detailed working plans.)

He is responsible for the source, colour, and intensity of every unit of *illumination*. This he sets out in his lighting-plot.

He is responsible for the *organization of arrangements behind the scenes*—for the stage manager's " property plot," for dressing-room arrangements, and for the choice and control of make-up.

[1] *e.g. Week commencing February , 19*

MONDAY . .	12.30.	Pish-Tush, Nanki-Poo, Pooh-Bah (trio, Act I.).
	4.15.	Katisha.
TUESDAY . .	12.30–1.45.	Men's Chorus. Nanki-Poo, Pish-Tush, Ko-Ko (opening numbers).
	4.45.	Yum-Yum, Pitti-Sing, Peep-Bo.
WEDNESDAY .		Morning break. Yum-Yum. (Solo, Act II.)
	12.30.	Mikado, Katisha, Ko-Ko, Pooh-Bah, Pitti-Sing. (Act II.)
	4.15.	Nanki-Poo, Yum-Yum.
	7.30.	Experimental lighting rehearsal.
THURSDAY .	12.30–1.45.	Full cast—Finale, Act I.
	4.45.	Ko-Ko, Katisha. (Duet and dance, Act II.)
FRIDAY . .	12.30.	Mikado, Katisha.
	4.15.	Nanki-Poo, Ko-Ko, Pooh-Bah, Yum-Yum, Pitti-Sing (for dance for " The flowers that bloom . . .").
SATURDAY .	9.30–12.	Girls' Chorus.
		Evening (time later). Three Little Maids.

He should have a voice, too, in the matter of *programmes* ; other " front-of-the-house " business—bookings, printing, and so on—should be some one else's responsibility.

The Qualities required in a Producer.—The first quality demanded of the producer, obviously, is some power of organization. However vague his ultimate ideas about the interpretation of the drama, his directions to those who work under him must be explicit and clear-cut. The slipshod producer is a pest.

Secondly, he needs (what a professional producer might get along without) teaching ability, including at least the normal share of its chief component—patience. The professional, who is handling accomplished actors, may find it sufficient to suggest a certain intonation ; the school producer, working with raw material, may not only have to say how he thinks the passage should be said, and explain *why* he thinks it should be said like that, but to demonstrate over and over again, until the young actor can, with understanding, incorporate the suggested inflexions and gestures naturally into his own self-expression. Similarly with movement.

Without these two qualities no school producer is likely to make an efficient job of his production. Whether it is any more than efficient depends upon his possession of other qualities which we are not called upon to analyse here, but it is in the assumption that he possesses some kind of artistic taste or sensibility that the producer is allowed to wield the dictatorship he enjoys in the modern theatre. Every one knows the passage in which Gordon Craig attributes the weakness of the old theatre to the number of head cooks who assisted to spoil the broth. " It is impossible for a work of art ever to be produced where more than one brain is permitted to direct ; and if works of art are not seen in the theatre this one reason is a sufficient one, though there are plenty more."

The Modern Idea of Production.—One cannot lay too much

stress on this importance of the production being conceived
as a whole through the imagination of a single mind. The
one certain way to make a performance in the worst sense
" amateurish " is to say to one man, " You rehearse," to
another, " You do the scenery," and to a third, " You do the
lighting." The producer might find himself having to play a
symbolic drama in a realistic setting ! Lighting and setting
contribute so integrally to the atmosphere of a play that they
cannot for a moment be considered as things apart. If play
presentation means, as a writer of the modern school has put
it, " the business of re-creating an author's vision for his
audience," there must be a controlling and co-ordinating
brain if there is to be any artistic unity and conviction about
the thing at all.

This is the central belief in the modern conception of the
theatre.

" A quarter of a century ago," says Selden, " the art of the
theatre was considered to be a composite thing, a large art
made by bringing together, for a moment, a number of loosely
related, independent, lesser arts. Sometimes the members of
this group co-operated in a performance, but more often they
competed against each other. To-day the art of the theatre
is better understood to be a single thing, a great art made out
of a complete fusion of many lesser arts."

It is a well-worn but useful simile that likens the producer
of a play to the conductor of an orchestra. He regulates the
tempo, he builds up the climaxes, he interprets the mood, he
suppresses the playing here and brings out the playing there,
he makes every component contribute just its proper share
to his conception of the whole work, and, by imposing unity
on diversity, achieves artistic creation. The producer of a
school play, it may not unfairly be added, has not only to
conduct the orchestra ; he has first to manufacture some of
the instruments (flood-boxes from old biscuit tins, for example),

and then to teach most of the instrumentalists the rudiments of playing.

The Producer and the Technical Side.—All this is not to suggest that the producer does every mortal thing with his own hands. He will naturally work in close conjunction with his colleagues in the various specialist departments which may be charged with the actual construction or painting of scenery, or the wiring and fixing of lights. (It need hardly be said that in his relations with his colleagues he will not order ; he will humbly suggest. Although his supreme responsibility must be understood, the instrument of his dictatorship must be tact.) The essential thing is that he should know what he wants. He may know nothing about practical electricity, but what he *must* know is what he wants his stage to look like when lit, and he has to make this as clear to the electrician as he can. Here a model stage will be helpful to him both for experiment and demonstration.

In the long run, however, it will pay the producer to master the practical details of every department of stagecraft, from the efficiency of fuses to the sizing of scene-canvas, for, as Harold Ridge points out, although he may employ others in his work, " he will be unable to command their respect or insist on his requirements being met unless he can instruct them in their work should it be necessary." He should learn all he can of established stage practice (it is sheer arrogance for the amateur to think that he can ignore the technical achievements of the commercial theatre because he dislikes its artistic policy), and make friends with the stage managers and carpenters and electricians of as many up-to-date theatres as he can. When he sees some striking effect in a stage performance let him secure permission—it will be readily forthcoming—to go " behind " and see how it is done. He will learn endless things which he can adapt for his own use. He cannot expect his colleagues in the handicraft and physics departments to spend their leisure picking up technical tips of this kind on the off-chance that they may one day serve to execute one of his whims. If the producer is going to specialize, let him "make a job of it." [1]

This technical knowledge will be all the more necessary if he employs professionals from outside, for, as Ridge again says, the average electrician knows little about stage requirements, and is deeply prejudiced by the routine of domestic lighting ; nor will it be a solution to engage Mr. Jones, assistant electrician at the local Theatre Royal, for not only is the lighting equipment of most provincial theatres hopelessly obsolete, but " it frequently happens that when some special lighting effect is wanted, the electrician, either through ignorance or laziness, declares it to be impossible. In such a case the producer should be able to instruct the electrician and draw any necessary wiring and switching diagrams. The same thing applies to the construction and working of scenery." [2]

The Producer and the Team Spirit.—One special responsibility, or opportunity, of the producer remains to be mentioned. It is notorious that some school shows, especially where staff participate, engender a certain amount of jealousy and bad feeling. Where so many nerves are on edge it is easy to understand. But there are other schools where the dramatic enterprise brings to birth a spirit of comradeship which, to those privileged to share it, makes the whole thing unforgettably worth while. The wise producer will do all he can, especially by his method of handling the performers at rehearsal, to prompt the feeling that they are all members of a team, all " good companions " together.

He might uphold to them the example of the Moscow Art

[1] See Gordon Craig's " Message to English Designers " in *Design in the Theatre* (*Studio*, 1927) : " Learn the whole thing, the whole technical theatre." And again in *The Theatre Advancing* : " You will never learn the Art until you are modest enough to desire to learn all about the humblest parts of the structure of theatres—scenery, costumes, and acting—and to learn it thoroughly."

[2] *Stage Lighting for Little Theatres.*

Theatre, or of the *Compagnie de Quinze*, whose methods suggest
M. Komisarjevsky's ideal theatre—" a laboratory for actors,
whose members work together for a long time, more or less
irrespective of productions, experimenting with new methods."
But both these teams have recognized the truth of Craig's
dictum that " until discipline is understood in a theatre to
be willing and reliant obedience to the manager or captain, no
supreme achievement can be accomplished." Indeed, some of
the " rules " of the Moscow Art Theatre might be adopted
by the School Dramatic Society :

> " All disobedience to the creative life of the theatre is a
> crime."

> " Lateness, laziness, caprice, hysteria, bad character,
> ignorance of the rôle, the necessity of repeating any-
> thing twice, are all equally harmful to our enterprise,
> and must be rooted out."

> " There are no small parts ; there are only small actors."

If the actors were absent or late they were fined. M.
Balieff, whose *Chauve-Souris* sprang from the Moscow Art
Theatre, declares that when touring he fines his players if
they are not at the station *one hour* before the train goes !
Yet a jollier team than his it would be hard to find.

The team spirit of such companies expresses itself in a
readiness to rehearse until perfection is obtained. M. Balieff
rehearses his players several mornings a week, even in numbers
which they have been playing regularly for ten years. (" In
England," he says, " you rehearse for three weeks, and then
run three hundred nights without rehearsing. If we run
three hundred nights we rehearse three hundred times.") In
the Moscow Art Theatre the players prepare themselves for
their parts by months of intense study—they may spend a
whole year on a production. If this attitude can be induced in the school society, rehearsals will not be regarded as
onerous.

The number of rehearsals necessary will vary with the nature of the work. Revue items may sometimes be arranged in three or four rehearsals ; for *The Mikado* the writer required one hundred and fifty (exclusive of musical preparation) ; for a full-length play eight weeks can be regarded as a minimum.

CHAPTER II.—REHEARSALS

1. The Producer's Preliminary Preparations

Imaginative Conception of the Play.—The first step in the production of any play—whether on the school stage or the stage of Sadlers Wells, or the Moscow Art Theatre—is the imaginative conception of the work as a whole. This conditions all the rest—settings, lighting, costumes, acting. It is through these things that the producer interprets to an audience the underlying purpose of the dramatist. He has first to make this purpose clear to himself, to saturate himself in the play until its spirit possesses him and he can instinctively *feel* what things are in keeping with its character and most likely to express its inner meaning. (If he finds no inner meaning there is either something wrong with him or with the play which he has chosen to present ; either he is not a suitable person to produce the play, or the play is unworthy of production by serious lovers of drama.) He may no more be able than the dramatist himself to sum up in a phrase this " inner meaning " ("intangible essence," as Professor Allardyce Nicoll calls it [1]), but the idea must fill his mind as it once did the dramatist's ; in a sense he must pass through the same ferment of creation as if he were making the play himself from the very beginning. The primary outfit of the producer must be " the seeing eye " of Carlyle's heroic poet—

---

[1] *Studies in Shakespeare.* (Hogarth Press.) The whole of Nicoll's introductory chapter is of great interest to the producer.

"the faculty which enables him to discern the inner heart of things, and the harmony that dwells there."

Full comprehension of the play may involve not only intensive study of the text, but wide reading of comparative and illustrative material. Probably no play can be fully understood apart from its author and its period. It is helpful to know not only the external considerations that affected its composition—for what kind of stage, and players, and audience it was written—but also the influences and ideas that were at work in the author's mind at the time. Understanding of *Hamlet*, for example, is deepened by a knowledge of the other works of Shakespeare's tragic period, and also (if less obviously) by acquaintance with the works of Kyd and Marlowe ; a producer will make a better job of *The Winter's Tale* or *The Tempest* if he knows the contemporary romantic comedy of Beaumont and Fletcher. Again, he may often obtain valuable clues by comparing a work with the sources from which it was derived, for when Shakespeare departed from what he found in Cinthio or North or Holinshed, it was usually for some significant reason. And when it comes to a modern play of ideas, the producer will read as much material on the same theme as he can get hold of. " I let my scenes grow," says Craig in a classic passage, " not merely out of the play, but from the broad sweeps of thought which the play has conjured up in me, or even other plays by the same author have conjured up. . . . We are concerned with the heart of this thing, and with loving and understanding it. Therefore approach it from all sides, surround it, and do not let yourself be attracted away by the idea of scene as an end in itself, of costume as an end in itself, or of stage management or any of these things, and never lose hold of your determination to win through to the secret—the secret which lies at the creation of another beauty." What does it matter if your conception is not the orthodox one ? It is yours for the time being, and the only one you can honestly attempt to realize in production.[1]

The Transition to the Stage.—Nevertheless, the producer needs to proceed to his first rehearsal with something more definite in his mind than a sense of vague exaltation. There comes a stage in all creative work when, as R. L. S. said, " the artist must step down, don his working clothes, and become the artisan." The producer must now think out the play in terms of the theatre ; he must visualize it scene by scene and line by line as it can be presented to a particular audience by particular players on a particular stage within the limitations imposed by particular means. He must have everything " cut and dried " before rehearsals start.

The producer who has filled his mind with the spirit of the play will, in fact, find the mechanical problems of production resolving themselves in his thought. At first he will find himself visualizing the play most clearly at certain key moments, climaxes, peaks of dramatic intensity. Later, when he comes to fill in the gaps, he may have to compromise with these initial visualizations if he is to secure a harmonious and smooth-flowing whole, but for the most part the production will be built around them. In plotting out stage positions, for instance, he will often find it best to work backwards—to group the characters as seems most fitting at certain critical or dramatic points, and then to trace back their movements to the time of their entrance.

Key Moments.—These " key moments " demand a word of comment. They are essentially of two kinds, emotional and intellectual. There are certain moments in the play when the minds of the audience are in a state of high tension. Between these moments tension is relaxed. The producer has to make

---

[1] " A fine play is capable of many interpretations. The producer must make his own interpretation, and subdue all else to that."—KOMISARJEVSKY in *Drama*, February 1926. Quoted by C. B. Purdom.

up his mind where the dramatist intends these emotional climaxes to come, and to work up to them. He also has to control their degree of intensity to ensure that a minor climax does not overshadow one more important, and that the architectural structure of the plot is not obscured. Indeed, this oscillation in emotional pitch is merely the rhythmic basis of a larger design. The design itself, leading up inevitably to the major climax, must be left clear. Bradley has pointed out the regularity with which this alternation of tension is employed in the plays of Shakespeare and his contemporaries.[1]

There are also moments in the play when what is said or done on the stage is of great importance if the audience is to grasp the full significance of the work. These are the passages that foreshadow what is to happen, or throw light on what has passed, or help somehow to illuminate the play's inner meaning, or underline the author's purpose. From the producer's point of view they are critical, and he must take special pains to see that they " get across."

The audience in the theatre is like a class in school—it cannot concentrate its attention for very long continuously. It " listens " only to a part of what it " hears." The producer must see to it that the audience does " listen " at these key points, and must work up to them accordingly. Again, his preliminary study of the play will indicate to him when they come. They may occur, especially during the early scenes, at times when the action is unexciting, but sometimes they will coincide with moments of emotional tension, and the conjunction frequently gives rise to the greatest passages of the play. From the union of intellect and emotion is born the soul.

Plotting Movements.—Before the first rehearsal the pro-

[1] It is interesting to develop Bradley's argument. Shakespeare, unhampered by scene-changes, sought variation mainly by an alternation of pitch between adjacent (usually short) scenes ; the modern dramatist, restricted by conventional notions of scenery, is forced to provide variety and relief within the framework of his (comparatively long) scenes ; the ultra-modern dramatist, replacing scenery by lighting, is reverting to the Shakespearean practice.

ducer will have sketched out the elementary mechanics of
entrances and exits and stage positions, perhaps with the help
of chessmen to represent his characters.[1] He must have
determined exactly where he is going to place his doors and
windows, his tables and chairs, or any other properties that
may affect the action.   Some of these arrangements he may
find it necessary to modify later, but clearly his early rehearsals
will be chaotic if the characters are left to wander about at
their own sweet will or come in by the right when the text, a
few minutes later, makes it apparent that they should have
entered by the left.[2]

In working out these positions the producer's constant aim
will be to give prominence where prominence is due ; the most
dominating figure on the stage should occupy, if possible, the
most dominating position (which will normally be somewhere
at the back of the stage in the middle—" Up Centre "—the
position from which the actor can command the whole stage
without having to turn away from the audience) ; figures
isolated from the others on the stage psychologically (*e.g.*
Shylock) should be separated spatially.   But we are anticipat-
ing a later section.

The Prompt-copy.—All these movements and positions
should be noted diagrammatically in the producer's prompt-
copy of the play.   To prepare this he should interleave his
printed text with blank pages (either rebinding it, or perforat-
ing it for loose-leaf fastening).   Another method (which requires two copies of the text) is to paste the printed pages into
a stout notebook so as to leave (in addition to marginal space)

[1] Some producers move these figures upon a model of the stage, but unless the
setting involves different levels, a plan-drawing showing the disposition of scenery
and furniture serves the purpose equally well.

[2] The instructions " Enter Up Right," or " Exit Down Left," etc., found in modern
plays, the producer must regard himself at liberty to ignore ; they were not devised
for his stage, and should not be allowed to cramp him ; he should work such things
out for himself.   Incidentally, " Left " and " Right " are used of the actor, not of the
audience ; " Down stage " means towards the footlights, " Up stage " away from
them.

a blank page opposite each page of print. The larger the cast the more important these preparations are.

Cutting.—Any cuts or alterations which are found necessary should be marked in the prompt-copy, which can act as a master-copy for reference by the players.

The amount of cutting which is legitimate varies inversely with the quality of the play. A certain provincial Repertory Company, performing light modern stuff, regularly cuts its plays by half an hour or more on Saturday evenings so as to cram in two performances, and it never seems to make much difference ; with well-knit plays this would be utterly impossible. Passages of great verse, of course, must be scrupulously respected, but it is not necessary to regard the entire text of Shakespeare as sacrosanct, for the simple reason that we do not know how much of it is Shakespeare's text at all. Some of the " probably spurious " scenes can be omitted, and perhaps some of the duller topical allusions.[1] Verse of any kind, if cut, must be clean cut, not mangled. The motive for cutting should always be dramatic, not commercial ; it should be done in the interests of the play, not in the interests of those who want to hurry away to catch trams and buses. If the retention of a dull or difficult scene or passage is likely (as presented on your stage) to hinder "the re-creation of the author's vision for an audience," then no service is being rendered to the author.

It is, perhaps, permissible to modify the wording of translations which have been unfelicitously or undramatically phrased. When the writer came to produce *R.U.R.*, he found that there were two versions of the play extant in English—one used for the London production, and the other for the New York production, each with merits and defects

---

[1] For some sound sense on this subject (as on others) see Granville-Barker's *Prefaces to Shakespeare* (*First Series*). " No hard and fast rule," he says, " will apply. Macbeth's porter's farmer and equivocator will never win spontaneous laughter again. But we cannot away with them, or nothing is left of the porter " (page xxxix.).

of its own. His knowledge of the Czechoslovakian tongue being inadequate to determine which text was nearer to Capek's original, he was forced—having received permission to collate the two versions—to judge every passage simply on the grounds of its theatrical effectiveness. All the proposed variants were fully debated at meetings of the leading players, who thus had the inestimable value of feeling that they were assisting in the very composition of the play.

According to Plan ?—While time spent in preparation is never wasted, producers vary in the degree to which they adhere to their original plans. I remember reading of a famous French producer who would not only spend far longer in preparing alone than in actually rehearsing, but who would never change a single thing at rehearsal on the grounds that the idea he evoked amid cool concentration was bound to be better than anything that could come out of the heat and clash of floor-work. On the other hand, there is sometimes revealed to the producer, as rehearsals proceed, a sudden inner significance in a certain line of phrase which he had not previously apprehended, and he has to devise ways and means of making this significance clear to the audience. Particularly with Shakespeare, one is constantly surprised at finding, perhaps only after several rehearsals, a hitherto unimagined significance in passages which have been familiar since childhood. The producer's approach to Shakespeare must always, it seems to me, be respectfully tentative.

Casting by Experiment.—If this is true, it is an interesting plan to let the various players try to act each other's parts, and to make suggestions as to how they should be played. The wise producer will weigh these suggestions with care, and while he alone is responsible for the interpretation which is decided upon, the actors will profit by the extension of their imaginative experience and by being made to ponder over the problems of the play, and their playing in their own parts should gain correspondingly in intelligence. The time spent, from their point of view, will not have been wasted. The commercial producer would certainly not consider this worth while, but the school producer sees the real justification of the time he devotes in the educative by-product of his labour.

By this interchange of players, furthermore, mistakes in casting may often be discovered. I remember a case where a lad assigned a minor part gave so original a reading when he was asked to take another character, that there was no option but to promote him, and in the end he had to be given the principal part, and the whole cast rearranged. Selecting the cast by trial and error is, of course, essential when a school is taking up dramatic work for the first time, but it is also worth while even when the producer is thoroughly familiar with his acting material ; otherwise there is the danger of a boy playing the same "type" all through his school career, and perhaps never expressing the best that is in him.

Another advantage of accustoming the players to read or act each other's parts is that it facilitates sudden rearrangements of cast in the case of illness. Few schools can afford to have one of their best actors immobilized as an understudy to the hero, and understudies to leading parts *must be* good actors. It is much better if the cast can be reshuffled and a new actor brought into some minor part. Here the school producer has an advantage over the Amateur Dramatic Society producer.

For my own part, when producing a play, and sometimes when trying to decide on the suitability of a play for production, I like to spend several floor-readings in ringing the changes on all the chief parts.[1] By the end of that time I have usually a clear idea of the cast I need, and I also find that ideas about the play and the playing have had time to crystallize in my

---

[1] A " floor-reading," as I have used the phrase, differs from a " rehearsal with texts," inasmuch as the producer's directions are tentative and are not written down by the players. Floor-readings of plays should be part of the regular activity of the dramatic society.

mind. These readings, of course, do not obviate the need for intensive study of the play.

New actors—provided always that there is reason to believe in their ability to bring some real personal quality to bear upon the part—should be persevered with as long as possible before they are dropped. For the first few rehearsals nervousness may inhibit their powers. Dignified members of the Sixth, for instance, will at first be extremely reluctant to " make fools of themselves " before the lower school members of the company by " going all out." Again, I can recall a case of a lad who, being gifted (so one judged from his classroom manner) as a natural clown, was given the part of Bottom in *A Midsummer Night's Dream*. For at least a dozen rehearsals he was hopeless and heartbreaking, but when the performances came he made a very big (and well deserved) hit in the part.

Acting ability is only one of the qualities that the producer will consider in casting. Different parts require different attributes. Some boys may be chosen for the quality of their speaking voices, others for their physical presence, others for their grace in movement, others for the imagined receptivity of their features to feminine make-up. Somewhere in the school will be the right player for every part. Part of the producer's success will depend on his *flair* for " spotting the supers." The " stars " will pick themselves.

Meeting the Cast.—Let us now assume that the producer has completed his preliminary cerebrations, and meets his cast—tentative or definite—for the first time. Many of the best professional producers make time to read the play over to the company themselves, trying to show by intonation, and perhaps occasional explanation, how it appears to them, at the same time expounding any difficult passages or archaisms, and laying down the standard of pronunciation of difficult or foreign names. The schoolmaster will sometimes have done this in the classroom—it depends upon the play and upon the spread of forms from which his cast is drawn—but it should on no account be omitted.   It is vital that the cast should see the play *as a whole* in their imagination before they come to act even the tiniest bit of it, and consequently all those who are likely to take a part—even all members of the dramatic society —should be invited to this meeting.   Questions and discussion may very profitably follow, and I believe that the producer should take the actors (and stage hands and electricians) into his confidence, and explain to them the lines along which he intends to work.   This will make much of his subsequent work far more intelligible to them.   He can describe, too, the settings he has in mind, and challenge members of the Stage-craft Guild (see Chapter X.) to work the designs out in detail, utilizing, as far as possible, the equipment already possessed by the company.   He may get some valuable suggestions as a result, but that is comparatively immaterial; his real purpose is to set as many boys as possible thinking about the problems of staging the play, and to make the whole thing appear a co-operative enterprise.   There is educational value in training producers as well as actors.   If the play is a long one, all this may take several meetings.   Then should follow a reading by the company, and, if required, the floor-readings described in a previous paragraph.   We now proceed to rehearsals proper.[1]

[1] *The Memorandum on the Teaching of English,* issued by the Association of Assistant Mistresses, says that amongst the mistakes to be avoided in preparing the school play is " dividing the coaching amongst too many people.   *It must be shared,* but by as few as possible, and those few in sympathy and agreed as to aims and methods."   The italics are mine.   From the point of view taken in this book, the " sharing " of " coaching " at all is inconceivable.   The same document suggests that a disadvantage of acting modern plays is that " the parts have been created by eminent living actors ; *neither producer nor audience can imagine any other interpretation.*"   Again I conceal my feeling in italics.—E. F. D.

2. Business and Grouping

The first few rehearsals should aim at taking the players right through the play, giving them their exits, entrances, and stage positions, and these they should note in their copies. (Let the producer insist on this.) Subsequent rehearsals will concentrate intensively on small sections of the play (sections involving the same players being conveniently taken together on the same occasion), though, as soon as possible, the sections should be linked together by a complete " run through " of the whole play, or at least of an Act, and as the time for the performance draws nearer these full rehearsals, conducted with a minimum of interruption, and preferably with criticism saved up for the end, should be held with increasing frequency. On these special occasions the producer should station himself at the back of the hall (where, incidentally, he can test audibility); for the rest, he should be in the thick of things on the stage itself, moving the players where he wants them, demonstrating, quietly explaining.

Rehearsal Stages.—Instruction at rehearsals should be cumulative. It is fatal to pile too much upon the actors at first ; let them make sure of one thing at a time and know why they are doing it. There is nothing more deadening than for rehearsals to be a succession of dreary drills ; each should contribute something new and definite towards the synthesis of the ultimate performance : first, positions and stage movements ; next, the meaning of the text as revealed by the expression of the spoken word, and by pauses (which should be noted in the texts—again, let the producer insist !) ; then (books having been dispensed with), gesture and the details of groupings ; then again, the taking up of cues and the regulation of pace ; and again, further refinements of expression and gesture, and, indeed, of all these things, until the skeleton acquires not only flesh and blood but a spirit, and springs into life.

Doing without Books.—The preceding passage suggests the appropriate time for discarding books. There should be no attempt to dispense with them before, and the actor should be positively discouraged from memorizing anything until it has been rehearsed. He will learn the lines more readily and intelligently when he can visualize his position on the stage, and when he knows the inflections which the producer requires. But clearly a time is reached when there can be no further progress while the players have books in their hands, and if this is pointed out to them there should be little difficulty about getting the parts learnt. Some discretion should be used in prohibiting books after a certain date—better a player with a book in his hand than one whose whole mind is absorbed by the effort to remember. If the producer states clearly in his weekly (or fortnightly) schedule of rehearsals the section of the play he proposes to treat on each occasion, he will find that most people come prepared.

The Players and the Settings.—From the very beginning the players should be told the exact positions of doors, windows, furniture, and other elements of the setting. The producer can show them the drawings and ground-plans for the various sets, and they will soon know exactly where to place forms and chairs to mark out the playing area on the platform. (When the producer arrives to take a rehearsal of any scene he should expect to find the stage " set " for it in this way.) If the play involves little change of scenery the outline of the scene can be indicated exactly by measured chalk lines, or by pinned tapes. (Always a useful check on one's ground-plans, as well as a help when the scenery is actually being erected.) These marks are especially helpful when the actual stage is not available for rehearsal. The more people participating in a scene the more essential it is that the playing area should be clearly defined. When we rehearse dance movements for opera—which need exact adjustment to the available space— we usually do it in our gymnasium, not on the stage, and there we have the stage boundaries and scenery positions marked upon the floor with strict accuracy. The result is that transfer to the stage and the introduction of scenery involve no dislocation. All the same, whenever possible, the scenery should be available for acting rehearsals some time before the show, to accustom the players to the manipulation of door handles and things of that kind. The whole idea is that the players should be so familiar with their artificial environment that they are free to seize it in their imagination as truth. Then they may be able to persuade the audience to accept it as truth too. The producer may help the players further if he explains to them how he hopes, by means of lighting, to achieve the mood or atmosphere of each scene. (See also p. 59 and Appendix II.)

The Introduction of Properties.—Steps and platforms on which the players have to be grouped should be available from the very beginning. Hand properties necessary for stage business (whether ducats, or fans, or teacups) should be introduced as soon as the actors can dispense with their books. Getting the details right gives the actor confidence.

Stage Business.—Some playwrights give ample directions for stage business ; Shaw, for example, gives us every detail, so that Craig is led to complain of his insolence in trying to tell Irving how to act.[1] Schoolboy actors, however, are not Irvings, and welcome all the help they can get in the interpretation of their lines. The producer must decide how much, if any, of the description with which Shaw and Barrie and others, with an eye on the reading public, inflate their plays *is* helpful ;

---

[1] Gordon Craig, *Henry Irving*. Dent. 1930. 15s.

usually the author's suggestions are best ignored.[1] Shakespeare, of course, (as distinct from his industrious editors) gives almost no direct instruction to the actor, and rehearsing his plays often resolves itself into inventing the directions which one imagines Shakespeare to have given orally to the original performers. But his text is rich in clues : " Look how she rubs her hands." " Good sir, why do you start ? " " You pulled me by the cloak." Many modern scholars follow Mr. Percy Simpson[2] in believing that Shakespeare used punctuation marks as a kind of code to indicate stage business, and Sir Arthur Quiller-Couch and Professor Dover Wilson have made fascinating use of this theory in their new edition of Shakespeare for the Cambridge University Press—an edition invaluable for producers.[3]

All stage business should have some definite purpose. There are on the market various " acting editions " which simply bristle with unnecessary business. The characters are perpetually " going up L." or " coming down R.," and usually for no reason at all. At times " they cross "—*i.e.* rise on a common impulse, prowl a turn each round the room and sit down in each other's chairs. All this, of course, is bad. If the producer thinks that his actors have been too long in one position he must invent some legitimate reason for moving them ; their movement must indicate restlessness, impatience, or at any rate a desire to fetch a pipe. But the value of repose is commonly underestimated. If people are more natural sitting still, leave them alone.

Incidentally, there is no reason why people should be allowed to sit only in modern plays. In too many performances

---

[1] *Cp.* Ashley Dukes in *The World to Play with* (Oxford. 1928. 6s.) : " A great number of supposed stage directions in the modern play are not stage directions at all, but commentaries and (literally) impertinences. . . . These weedy masses of italics should be burned in one heap, and their ashes applied to nourishing the roots of dramatic speech " (page 107).

[2] *Shakespearean Punctuation.* 1910.

[3] *Cp.* the quotation from Roy Mitchell on page 60.

of Shakespeare the actors never sit down—unless it be upon a throne ; they merely walk on and off the stage for the purpose, it seems, of delivering recitations ! Remember that if the actors appear uncomfortable, their discomfort will communicate itself to the audience.

The Curse of Fidgeting.—One of the hardest things to teach young actors is not to fidget. Movements must be definite and deliberate, and for the rest the actors *must keep still.* (Stanislavsky vividly describes how he disciplined himself to keep his body still, clenching his hands till the nails drew blood, pressing his toes with all his weight into the floor till blood was left in his shoes !) Those who have least to say in a scene sometimes require the most rehearsal, for they must be engaged naturally, but not so as to distract attention from the principals.[1] They must neither fill in the interval of waiting for their next cue by trying to spot sister Mary in the stalls (a practice which offers the only sound argument for strong footlights !), nor must they, in the diligence of their attention to the play, turn expectantly to look at the next speaker before he actually opens his mouth to begin his speech.

Eyes.—It is by no means always necessary for the other characters to look at the speaker ; it depends on how they are reacting to what is being said. They must, of course, show by their expression that they are *listening.*[2] But the eyes of the audience follow the eyes of the actors, and this enables the astute producer to direct attention where he wants it. An obvious instance is where some one enters with some important piece of news—naturally he is the focal point of every eye on

[1] Unless, of course, the principals are so bad that you are forced to divert attention from them. Jeffreys (page 38) gives an interesting instance of bad acting in a school production being " covered " by amusing by-play.

[2] " Each character must show by his reactions precisely what the effect is upon him personally, as distinct from the other characters. . . . Whenever a speech is made upon the stage it is not made solely by the one who speaks the words, but by all the others who help to make it with their reactions."—EDWARD LEWIS, *The Producer and the Players*, pages 42, 44.

the stage. Less obviously, when a character is speaking a passage which has special significance, it will help to focus the attention of the audience if the other characters watch him attentively as he says it. Nor need eyes be focused necessarily on the speaker—they may, as it were, project the thoughts prompted by the speaker's words, directing attention to some particular object or person or place. An extremely good example is afforded by a production of *The Merchant of Venice* by one of Mr. Eric Barber's groups of village players in County Durham. During Portia's speech about " The quality of mercy " the eyes of all the players were bent, not upon Portia, but upon Shylock, so that what was passing in his mind was made the real centre of interest, and the audience waited anxiously for his response to her appeal. An opposite effect was secured in the production of *St. Joan* by the People's Theatre of Newcastle-on-Tyne. In the cathedral scene, when Joan realizes at last that she is alone on earth, her listeners were made to stand with averted faces, emphasizing both her isolation and their shame. Attention was diverted from Joan to the others. Possibly, in this instance, La Hire might have been permitted to gaze at Joan during her outburst, preparing the audience for his vigorous reaffirmation of belief in her.

In Plate 10 (*R.U.R.*, Act III.) one figure holds the attention of the other four men who are standing ; the woman, for whom the words he speaks have a dreadful personal significance, is staring ahead ; the character seated on the right has observed her agitation.

It is a common fault of young actors to regard their boots. In everyday life people look at those to whom they speak, and as a general rule they should do the same on the stage. But the exceptions to the rule will be significant—and will carry significance. Avoidance of another's glance may indicate an uneasy conscience, or the speaker (as in grief) may be entirely self-absorbed, or (as in inspiration) may be seeing only his visions, or (as in determination) may be thinking more of what he is saying than of the person to whom he is saying it.[1]

When two characters are conversing it is usual to place them close together ; if they are on opposite sides of the stage the audience soon develops " Wimbledon neck," and grows tired. But if you want to stir the spectators up to sudden excitement you can do much by compelling their eyes to leap rapidly from one point of the stage to another. The value of this device depends on its being used sparingly and against a background of repose.

Grouping : (*a*) **Masking.**—The producer's first care in his grouping of the characters must be the avoidance of " masking " —the hiding of some players by the movements of others : a bad fault in many school productions. Obviously, there are occasions when everybody on the stage cannot be in view of the audience at once, but the main protagonists must stand out clearly, and there should be an uninterrupted view of the speaker from every part of the hall. This calls for careful arrangement of playing positions, for it will not do merely for the speaker to burst forth from a crowd for the purpose of making his speech, or for those in front of him suddenly to step aside that the audience may see him. Anything so obvious must be avoided. The normal movement of the play should bring the players naturally into the appropriate positions at the appropriate times. The producer must be on the look-out for masking which occurs through players straying slightly from their allotted positions—a fault which may creep into a production at the last minute, and even necessitate special

[1] " You have a story to tell ; let your eye visualize the thing you speak. The public will see it reflected there. That is why, by the way, you cannot make a narrative speech in profile. Start it like that, facing your listener. Good ; but little by little turn, until at last you face your public ; your eye fixes itself on a point from which it does not move because it is there that you see what you are describing. That fixture of the eye carries the public panting after your words. What you are about to say they see there, before you utter it, and speech, in a measure, does no more than drive home the impression which the glance has already fixed in the attention of the spectator."—CoQUELIN.

[*Photo by Ladislaw.*]

PLATE I.—*The Road to Emmaus.* " And there was famine in the land.... "
Moira House School, Eastbourne.

Note in this and Plate XII. the simplicity of setting and beauty of pose and grouping.

PLATE II.—*Heraclius* at the Cambridge Festival
Theatre.
Produced by Herbert Prentice.
Illustrating asymmetrical grouping.

rehearsals after one or more public performances have been given.

(*b*) **Focusing Interest.**—But this is merely the negative side of grouping ; as a positive element in the production it can be one of the most eloquent of the means of expression at the producer's command, for grouping can be made both pictorially pleasing and dramatically significant, line and mass contributing to the mood of the scene and focusing attention to the centre of interest. When working with a few figures it is interesting to aim at a right-angled triangle formation, with the footlights representing the hypotenuse, and the central figure placed at the right angle ; the other two sides of the triangle, the other players, leading the eye to rest at the important point. Sometimes the right angle may be swung over from " Up Centre Left " to " Up Centre Right," as the centre of interest changes. And sometimes the angle will be obtuse and sometimes acute.

The triangular formation will not always be appropriate. The basis of all drama is conflict, and when the conflict can be resolved in terms of *dramatis personæ* it is sometimes possible to emphasize it by distinguishing the two sets of protagonists spatially on opposite sides of the stage.

Thus all good grouping is symbolic—" creating certain lines of force tending to interpret the idea of the play." Roy Mitchell gives some interesting examples applying this conception to certain scenes from Shakespeare's plays.

(*c*) **The Stage Picture.**—This talk of " sides of triangles " and " lines of force " does not mean that where many characters are on the stage together they should be allowed to stand about in straight rows. Nothing looks worse—unless it be a crowd arranged in concentric semicircles. The more characters there are upon the stage the greater the producer's opportunity to arrange them in a manner that, while appearing natural, is pictorially interesting and theatrically dynamic.

With large casts he must avoid the photographer's wedding-breakfast group; and with small casts, what Eric Barber calls " mantelpiece grouping—two vases, two whatnots, and a clock." He should aim at balance rather than exact symmetry. Plates I. and II. afford fine examples. And he should remember that his picture is in constant motion—a change of positions at one side of the stage may upset the balance of the whole, and call for some compensatory (but unobtrusive) adjustment of positions on the other side. In some productions, of course, grouping can be purely formal and abstract. The chorus of a Greek play or (in different fashion) of a Sullivan opera lends itself to treatment of this kind.

While the outlines of pictorial grouping will be designed by the producer in his study, the allocation of positions to various individuals can best be arranged on the stage itself. The heights of the players must be considered. (And, if possible, the producer will not place a weak tenor amidst a knot of strong basses !) Once the grouping has been determined, the players must rigidly observe their positions.

A *flair* for grouping will enable the producer to lift many a scene out of the commonplace, and stamp it unforgettably upon the imagination of his audience. He should practise and experiment with it for its own sake. An example of a scene depending almost entirely on grouping is given on pages 179–180.

(d) **Crowds.**—Crowd scenes need intense preparation. An actual mob on the stage will not look like a mob at all. Every member of it must know exactly when and where to move, and a plentiful use of chalk marks is recommended. (Guide marks placed near the footlights are frequently used in musical shows on the professional stage.) Granville-Barker once startled London by the crowd scenes in *Julius Cæsar* ; actually his " mob " was organized into groups, with a dozen section leaders to stage-manage the booing and cheering.[1] On the other hand the writer once witnessed a school production in which the lines " Revenge! About! Seek! Burn! Fire! Kill! Slay! Let not a traitor live!" were delivered in rhythmic unison!

The school producer *ought* to do better with crowd scenes than his colleagues on the professional and amateur stages. The professional manager usually cannot afford the cost of engaging large numbers and of spending time in drilling them; in amateur societies it is difficult to assemble any considerable body of players for regular rehearsal—particularly for non-speaking parts. But the school producer has both the material and the opportunity to train it. Crowd scenes on school stages should be the best in the modern theatre.

(*e*) **Stage Levels.**—Grouping is helped enormously if the flat platform of the stage can be diversified with raised terraces and steps. Different levels both diminish the dangers of masking, and increase the possibilities of decorative and—still more—symbolic treatment. The use of this device of the broken stage—from the early experiments of Appia down to the sectional stage lifts of *Cavalcade* and the new Stratford playhouse—forms one of the most interesting chapters in the story of the modern theatre. A study of some of the more famous designs will show how the *avant-garde* of continental producers love to mass their figures significantly upon different planes—often arranging them in triangular blocks, with each apex as a point of attention, and emphasizing the whole design by controlled lighting.

The advantage of levels is well illustrated in Plates I., II., and XII. Even the neo-realistic setting in Plate X. (*R.U.R.*, Act III.) affords a modest example, for there is a slight platform or dais at the rear of the stage. Time after time during the action this served to diversify grouping, or help

[1] *Cp. Coriolanus* at Stratford. Critique published in *Manchester Guardian*, April 26, 1933.

a character into momentary prominence. Of course, characters must not mount such a platform as though they were orators ascending a pulpit ; it must all be arranged unobtrusively.

3. The Actor and his Movements

Exits and Entrances.—Stage movements should anticipate exits. Rather than let a player discharge all his final speech on one side of the stage and then negotiate an embarrassed way to the opposite exit, split his speech up with movement, so that he is sufficiently near his exit for the final phrase to " take him off." (For a processional exit—e.g. of a king—the long, cross-stage movement would, of course, be admirable.) As a general rule the actors should not speak while actually walking about—particularly on improvised stages where the floorboards creak. Movements and words should be judicially interspersed.

Entrances can be made more effective occasionally if some of the characters on the stage look out into the wings as if they saw the new arrival approaching, thereby directing the eyes of the audience to the entrance, and helping to maintain the illusion that the wings represent a real extension of the stage landscape. This is often appropriate in performances of Shakespeare. Obviously it cannot be practised in a box set. It is a useful old stage rule which says that when two people enter in conversation the first to speak should enter second ; he has not then to look over his shoulder at the person he is addressing.

Perhaps this is the most appropriate place to call attention to Shakespeare's practice in marking entrances. An entrance in Shakespeare would seem to mean entrance upon the open platform of his stage, not necessarily into that portion of it occupied by the protagonists. On our modern stage Shakespeare's " enter " can be read quite often as simply a warning cue ; the actual entrance will be made perhaps some lines later. Thus Brutus will say " Here comes his body, mourned by Mark Antony " *before* (and not after, as in the text) the entrance of " Antony and others, with Cæsar's body " ; Banquo will say, " Give me my sword. Who's there ? " when he hears Macbeth's footsteps, not after his entrance. Examples could be multiplied indefinitely. Shakespeare's cues, as written, are only appropriate for a performance without scenery in the open air.

The More Interesting Side of the Actor.—Turning on the stage is frequently an awkward business—in many cases, I believe, because of too rigid insistence upon the old (and generally sound) rule that the actor must never turn his back upon the audience. So we see some one who is prowling round the stage in a natural left-hand wheel break it by an ugly right-hand turn, when the natural thing would be for him to continue his turn in the direction of his walk ! The producer should not be afraid of making a character stand or speak with his back to the audience, provided the action of the play warrants it and the actor can make himself heard. But it is not a sign of emancipation to make your actors play mainly to the back-cloth. With rare exceptions the front view of an actor is the more interesting ; many of the traditional " rules " of stage technique are based on the elementary principle that the actor should " uncover " as much of himself to the audience as possible.

Thus, if he is standing sideways, his up-stage foot will be slightly farther advanced than the other, so that his body is inclined down stage towards the audience (his weight, incidentally, on the down-stage foot) ; if he has to move he will start off with the up-stage foot first (really a half-step, transferring the weight preparatory to a full step with the other foot) ; if he has to kneel, he will sink on the down-stage knee (or on that knee first if he is going down on both knees) ; if he has to embrace a lady he will use his up-stage arm to get the major purchase upon her ; if he has to point, he will do it with his up-stage hand (unless it looks hopelessly left-handed), because the other would cramp his body.

A great deal can be learnt from watching the way in which experienced actors move and sit. We have already described the stance of the actor who is standing sideways to the audience. When he is facing the audience he will again stand with one foot slightly advanced, but this time his weight will be back on his up-stage foot. The secret of sitting down without awkwardness is to take the weight of the body on the foot nearer the chair as the body is lowered.[1]   Falls on the stage should be whole-hearted. They do not hurt if the body is relaxed.

Useful hints can often be found in the published memoirs of actors. Here is an interesting passage in Stanislavsky's *My Life in Art*, describing how he first came to play the part of an old man : " I was a bit prepared for the playing of old men. While I had practised before the mirror in our city house I had played everything, an old man included. Besides, I watched and imitated one of the old men I knew. Then I began to feel physically in myself that the normal state of an old man resembles the state of a young man after long exhaustion. The feet, the hands, the spine become wooden. Before rising, one must get ready to bend the body forward in order to move the centre of weight, to find a fulcrum, and to rise with the aid of the hands, for the legs half refuse to serve. On rising, you do not straighten out the back at once, but you unbend it gradually. Until the legs stretch, you walk with small steps, and only after a time begin to move

---

[1] *Cp.* M. V. C. Jeffreys : " Do not sit with both feet together, and the back square-on to the chair, and go down with a bump. Approach the chair obliquely, take the weight on the foot nearest the chair (quite close to it), pivot on that foot, and control the descent, bringing the other foot forward. Sit, and have done with it ; do not squirm about like a dog in its basket."

swiftly, but then it is hard to stop yourself " (page 156). And he goes on to tell how, when he came to put this into his part at rehearsal, he was admonished for over-acting. Nevertheless, " conscious relation to action that was typical of old age guided me, and as a result I tuned my own feelings to the physiological phenomena of senility. This created a kind of method from the outer to the inner, from the body to the soul, based upon an unbreakable bond between physical and psychical nature. All these technical means, although they did not create the image, prepared the soil for it " (page 182).

Gesture again.—On the subject of gesture it has been well said that it must be " full, open, uninhibited, however small the stage. Movement and gesture must on no account be reduced in scale to fit the stage, for the simple reason that the actor himself cannot be diminished. On a small stage movements must be reduced in *number*, not in *size*." [1] Let arm movements proceed from the shoulder, not the elbow. Gesture, of course, should fit the type of play ; in modern plays arm movements must be severely restrained ; in " costume " plays they may be more exaggerated, and in such plays the pictorial and decorative qualities of gesture may sometimes be usefully exploited. Gesture for purely dramatic purposes should only be resorted to when meaning or emotion cannot be adequately expressed without its aid. It must always be sincere ; it must never appear super-added. As a continuous sleight-of-hand accompaniment to blank verse, for example, it is utterly detestable. Gesture must never degenerate into gesticulation.[2]

---

[1] M. V. C. Jeffreys in Armstrong College Education Papers, Vol. III., No. 5, 1931.

[2] " Gesture is one of the weakest features of amateur acting. Those feeble little pushings out of the hands, with the elbows tight to the sides ; tentative, broken, clumsy, ugly movements which mean nothing and effect nothing ; that forefinger pointing, heaven knows why, towards the nether regions ; that clenching of the fists held rigidly a few inches away from the thighs ; those hands perpetually in the pockets, or perpetually behind the back, or moving from one position to the other by irritating clockwork ; those extended hands with the fingers all spreadeagled."— EDWARD LEWIS, *The Producer and the Players.*

Remember Hamlet's advice : " Do not saw the air too much with your hand . . . but use all gently."

Gestures illustrating speech should normally precede the words they emphasize. A demonstration will show, for example, that if you are ordering some one to leave the stage it is more effective to point the arm to the exit and then say, " Get out," than it is to say the words first and point afterwards. Gesture and words should arise together naturally in the actor's mind, born of the same emotion. The gesture lends sincerity to the words. But if it follows the words, it looks like an afterthought and is an anti-climax.

Period Gestures : Curtsies and Snuff.—1. For an ordinary curtsy the right foot is advanced, and the left leg carried behind the other to the right until the outside of the left knee rests against the inside of the right calf. The left knee can be lowered as far as is required.

2. For the eighteenth-century curtsy the body is lowered and the front leg is stretched out straight at the conclusion of the movement. There is the same initial sway forward, advancing the right foot, and then the left leg is carried away behind the right, fairly well extended, knee resting on the floor, and the whole body sinks back while the front leg is straightened. The beginning of the rise is the drawing-in of the front leg.

3. For the Elizabethan curtsy the right leg is advanced as before, and the left either slid back under the body or else taken back in a sweeping semicircular movement away from the body to the left, and the body lowered until it is sitting on the left heel. In this case the left knee does not touch the floor. Finally the front leg is straightened as before.

With appropriate dresses these exercises look more comfortable and graceful than they feel.

To take snuff with an air, hold the box delicately in the left hand, flick it open with the right, take snuff (real or imaginary) between thumb and forefinger of right hand, shake off surplus

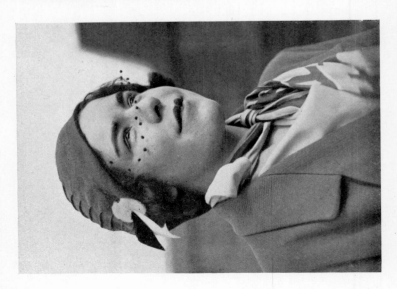

[*Photos by Author,*

PLATE III.—Two boys as girls—without " make-up."

by a series of wrist movements carrying the hand across to the right side of the body, sniff first at one nostril then at the other, with an intermediary flick and one or two final flourishes to dispose of remnants. Close box, take lace handkerchief hanging at left wrist and daintily flick away (real or imaginary) particles on the sleeve or coat. In doing all this beware of the gentle art of burlesquing your own action ! In other words, don't overdo it. But let the movements be free and sweeping, not cramped and fidgety. The eighteenth century had no trains to catch.

Boys in Girls' Parts.—Boys usually play girls' parts incomparably better than girls of the same age, and there is often an indefinable quality about their performance—a kind of wistful beauty—that makes one wonder whether Shakespeare was really handicapped by having no professional actresses to play his parts.

Boys playing girls' parts need special training in feminine " deportment." They must learn to walk with smallish steps, to move gracefully from the hips (back straight, chest lifted, head high, stomach in—which won't look at all graceful at first) ; in sitting, not to cross the legs, to keep the knees together (one foot slightly in advance of the other), and to remember the masking function of the skirt ; and with the hands, to keep the fingers close together (and, if the illusion of slenderness be further sought, the thumbs concealed [1]), to utilize the lap occasionally for resting, to avoid fidgeting with fans or handkerchiefs—comforting as these are to unoccupied hands—and to avoid feeling for a trousers pocket that is no longer there. They should have practice in moving about in women's clothes and with women's shoes for some time before the show ; they can well do this at home under maternal criticism and correction.

[1] A hint for which I am indebted to a copy of *Woman and Beauty*, which once furnished my sole reading matter in a moorland inn.

Boys cannot be taught to move gracefully in a few weeks ; the grooming process requires years. In the writer's experience the biennial performance of comic opera in his school has been of great assistance : all his leading " girl " actors have graduated " through the chorus " ; the modern Helena of his *R.U.R.* owed much of his grace to an earlier year's " schooling " as a " little maid," and even the burlesque dancing troupe described on page 181—which began simply as a *jeu d'esprit*— has helped to assure a constant supply of boys capable of moving without excessive awkwardness.

There is seldom need for boys to stop playing women's parts when their voices break ; a low " soft " tone, which they can often attain, is indeed the pleasantest quality to find in a " female " voice upon the stage.

Girls in Boys' Parts.—The writer leaves this section to be filled in by those better qualified than himself. He only ventures to anticipate an introductory sentence :

" Girls usually play boys' parts incomparably better than boys of the same age. . . ."

4. *Speaking the Words*

" It is on articulation that the actor must concentrate his first effort ; here is at once the A B C and highest achievement of our art."

COQUELIN.

The traditional injunction that " children should be seen and not heard " is, unfortunately, too often obeyed upon the school stage. The school producer will find that he has to spend a considerable amount of time teaching the actors to be (*a*) audible, (*b*) intelligible. This means that he has (*a*) to teach them to produce their voices properly; (*b*) to correct faulty enunciation.

Voice Production.—If voice production has been a regular part of speech training in the classroom, the producer's task will be much lightened.[1] He will then have merely to help his players to adjust the throw of their voices to the size of the hall. (He will find that voices which do not " carry " in an empty hall become perfectly audible when the audience is seated, and experience will show him how much allowance to make for this. Halls differ greatly in their acoustics.) The technique of voice production lies beyond the scope of this book. The two main elements, of course, are correct breathing and correct placing of the voice in the mouth. The voice must be supported on breath controlled from the very base of the lungs, and then placed well forward in the mouth so that full advantage is taken of the various resonating cavities in the head. Shrillness, shouting, and hoarseness are signs that a player is using only the top part of his lungs, and speaking from the throat. The young actor has constantly to be told to " keep the voice down " ; it will help him to do it correctly if you tell him to " pull in the stomach till it pushes the voice against the top teeth."

A properly produced voice has wide range and flexibility ; [2] it can penetrate without strain (even in a whisper) to all parts of the auditorium, and (above all) it has that pleasantness of quality that makes speech interesting to those who have to listen. Its modulations can convey the appropriate degree of dramatic tension ; " the sudden drop in the voice from *forte* to *piano* has the power of accentuating and thrilling the audience as much as the crescendo from the *piano* into the *forte*." [3] And it makes possible the expression of emotion ; even laughter and sobbing are matters of breath control.

[1] See page 170.
[2] " To make a long, balanced Shakespearean sentence sound simple and sincere, one has often to use a compass of at least two octaves, and to carry in one's head a melodic intonation as long as the Preislied, filled from end to end with harmonic intonations and fine shades of tone quality, emphasis, and phrasing."—Mr. LEWIS CASSON. Quoted by C. B. Purdom.
[3] Craig, *On the Art of the Theatre*, page 9.

Articulation.—The intelligibility of speech is more a matter of articulation—of the correct use of teeth and lips. Clipping and slurring are the two worst faults. Words must be clearly rounded off, and all consonants clearly articulated. (Vowels, from the point of view of the audience's hearing what is said, are less important.) Lingering over final consonants, which sounds artificial on the stage itself, will not be noticed from the hall unless it is overdone.[1] The final words of a sentence are very apt to pass into nothingness ; they must be given their full weight. The actor must avoid both the sloppiness of everyday speech and the excesses of the old-time " elocutionist." " The theatre," said Coquelin, " is not a drawing-room. We must not talk as we talk every day ; we must *speak*, with truth and naturalness—then it will be good speech, but still speech. . . . Chatting is not enough ; emphasis on diction at every point is too much. Truth lies between the two. The essential thing is to be understood."

Pace.—Many of these faults arise through the young actors trying to speak too quickly. The effect of pace is secured, not by gabbling but by staccato delivery and by the quick taking up of cues. When an actor (or a public speaker) perceives that he is not " getting over," the great temptation is for him to go faster, whereas the trouble often is that he is already going too fast for the audience to take in what he says. " When you say to yourself, ' Heavens, how slow I am ! Shall I ever get through ? This must be unutterably tedious,' then only are you beginning not to go too fast." [2]

What is fatal is unnecessary deliberation over unimportant lines. Professional players speak of " throwing away " the more or less irrelevant words, so that when they come to a line which it is vitally important for the audience to grasp, they

---

[1] Lingering over a final consonant does not mean adding an extra vowel. It is one thing (as Jeffreys points out) to sustain the *n* in " men " ; it is another to remove the tongue from the teeth, allow more breath to escape, and produce " menna."

[2] Related of Régnier by Coquelin.

can give it emphasis by taking it somewhat more deliberately.

Emphasizing a Word.—Essential words are best emphasized,
not by shouting but by a barely perceptible pause before
delivery. This is so important that it is placed in a paragraph
of its own.

Timing Laughs.—Boy actors, at first, want to speak too
soon—they won't wait till they are properly on the stage, or
till the last sentence has had its full effect. Many a laugh is
smothered because it is not waited for; [1] and players must be
warned in rehearsal when to expect laughs and not to speak
through them—though, of course, they must not wait till
every straggling echo has died away, or the scene will soon be
killed. (Players soon get to know the appropriate moment
to resume, but they may be disconcerted at first, and it is worth
while trying to assemble some audience for the dress rehearsal.
While the laugh is " on " the scene must be " frozen," as the
professionals say—there must be no movement ; the whole
action of the play is, as it were, suspended for a few seconds,
and it must resume as it left off, or the audience will be aware
of the convention.)

Silences.—Pauses are as important as speech. They give
to speech its due weight. They allow time for words to work.
And sometimes for gestures and movements to work. They
often become the most intense moments of the play. But
they must always have real significance, always dramatic
purpose. The audience must never wonder " What on earth
is everybody waiting for ? " It is very hard to persuade boys
to respect the pauses you deem to be necessary ; the only
way seems to be to make them count so many seconds to
themselves, or say some sentence under the breath, and

---

[1] *Cp.* " The laugh doesn't come straight on top of the joke. It's always joke—
silence—then bang—ha ! ha ! ha !—the roar comes back at you."—JACK HULBERT,
Observer, June 11, 1933.

even then the pauses tend to get shorter at succeeding re-hearsals.

Tempo.—The regulation of *tempo*—the adjustment of playing-pace to the dramatic rhythm of the play and the building up of climaxes—will be a major preoccupation of the producer at the later rehearsals. Variations of pace, as we have seen, are obtained mainly, not by variations in the rate of verbal delivery (though the rate may be far from uniform), but by variations in the speed of cue-taking.

" Cutting-in " needs careful rehearsal ; it is fatal if a player has to hang on to a word waiting to be interrupted. He should be given some words in continuation of his sentence that he can say if the other fellow is late with his interception ; this will minimize the risk of his being left suspended, as it were, in mid-air, and will make the interruption seem more natural.

Pitch.—Attention should be paid to the pitch of voice employed ; its variations may contribute to the emotional pattern. Quarrel passages, or exciting interchanges, for example, should start at a low pitch of tone and work up to a high one. On the other hand, a sudden drop in pitch is one of the surest ways of giving emphasis to a particular passage.

Pronunciation.—No mention has been made of pronuncia-tion because it is outside the scope of the producer's duties. He cannot hope in a few weeks to change the habits of his actors' lifetimes ; all that he can do is to correct odd sounds here and there, and lay down a standard for controversial words. (The B.B.C. publications, *Broadcast English*, 1928, and the supplementary lists, will be found helpful.) If a school wishes its pupils to have command of the " received standard " of English speech, it will make provision in its syllabus accordingly. The question of dialect is discussed in Chapter I.

5. *The Art of Acting*

" But what about the study of acting ? "

" My dear madam, do you suppose that we should attempt to teach that which every one has told us is unteachable ? Miss Ellen Terry has said that acting is not to be taught, and many others have said so too, and we are entirely of their opinion. It cannot be taught.

" But what *can* be taught is this : how to walk from one side of the stage to the other ; but that is moving, that is not acting. You can be taught how to move arms, legs, and torso with expression ; but that is not acting—that, again, is moving. You can be taught how to move your face ; you can even be taught how to move your soul—or rather, how to allow your soul to move you—but this is still not acting. That comes under the head of movement. Then you can be taught how to produce your voice so that it reaches to every part of the building and into the soul of the listener. You can be taught how not to speak ; but all this is not acting, it is speaking."

GORDON CRAIG, *The Theatre Advancing*, page 227.

" Feeling " a Part.—So far we have been discussing not acting but the externals of acting. Acting involves something more than stage technique. There may even be acting where there is no stage technique, though it is acting under a handicap. Technique merely increases the capacity of the actor to express himself, but he has first to have something to express. He has first to " feel " his part.

Whether—in the terms of the age-old controversy—the actor actually " lives " his part while he acts it, or whether he stands aloof and watches himself merely simulating emotions, is immaterial.[1] The emotions must have been, *at some time or other*, a real part of his personal experience. Otherwise, technique or no technique, he would be unable to convey them to his audience.

But will the schoolboy " feel " a part, so to speak, off his own bat ? Caldwell Cook says somewhere that " nothing but real experience can enable us to read a meaning into words."

[1] For a discussion of the controversy as it affects boy actors, see Appendix II.

The emotional experience of the schoolboy is limited ; he will
often fail to realize for himself the full significance of his lines.
None the less he is quick to realize that significance when it
is suggested to him in terms he can understand.   His imagination is alert and sympathetic, and he can apprehend emotional
states that have formed small part of his own experience.   He
can imagine, for example, the feeling of bereavement without
having suffered bereavement himself.   The producer's job is
to help the young actor to " feel " the part he is called upon
to interpret.

He has first to help him to understand the meaning of his
words.   Many producers, including some famous professional
producers, *paraphrase* difficult sections of the play, sometimes
even making the actors speak the paraphrase for a time instead
of the text, until they realize exactly what they are supposed
to be saying, and their gestures do seem to proceed from some
inner urgency—as gestures should.   The producer will also
discuss the character with the player (in a colloquial, not an
academic way), and try to suggest the mental states that
prompt the words.   (*e.g.* " You are such and such a fellow.
You have just been through such and such an experience.
The words come to you almost involuntarily ; you are thinking
of so and so as you say them," etc.)   The actor, once more,
must not only *understand* his part, he must *feel* it.   It is not
enough to tell the actor to " look frightened " when he sees
Banquo's ghost ; it is not enough (though it may be very helpful and stimulating, and the producer must not funk it) to
demonstrate how you would act it yourself ; you must try to
picture to him all that is passing through Macbeth's mind at
that terrible moment, so that he *is* Macbeth and he *is* frightened.
And only when he has lived through the part in that way need
he think about what gestures he ought to mechanize.   It is
here that drama educates imagination.   " It is the producer's
business not to prescribe certain movements, but to help the

[*Photo by Gillman, Oxford.*

PLATE IV.—*Hamlet,* by the Radley College A.D.S.
Produced by A. K. Boyd.
Settings designed by P. M. Simpson.

[*Photo by Gillman, Oxford.*

PLATE V.—The graveyard scene from the
Radley College *Hamlet*.

actor to experience the right feeling ; not to manipulate the
actor's face and limbs, but to administer the right emotional
stimulus." Acting, after all, must be creative, not imitative.
The schoolboy may welcome his master's demonstrations at
first ; the justification of them comes when they are no longer
needed.[1]

We have instanced *Macbeth*, but what has been said applies
equally to the part of a butler or clown. The emotional states
are simpler, but they must be experienced before they can be
acted. (Indeed, the writer is by no means convinced that
the effort to experience such complicated and sometimes
morbid emotional states as those of Macbeth is a healthy
exercise for adolescents at all. But the problem of such exceptional parts will only arise in the case of exceptional
actors.) The amount of help which the producer must give
will, of course, vary with the individual. Some imaginations
are more sluggish than others. The writer showed the MS. of
the previous paragraph to a sixteen-year-old boy actor. His
comment was, " Pretty rotten actor, sir, if the producer has
to do all that for him." He, though he knew it not, was an
exception.

In the actual performance the most emotional scenes need
to be the simplest. But it is wise to let the actors go " all
out " at rehearsal until they have felt themselves into their
parts, and to tone things down afterwards.

The Explanatory Paraphrase.—The device of the explanatory paraphrase referred to above is worth a moment's
elaboration. A player often misses the right expression
because he fails to grasp the meaning. A Cæsar who can make

---

[1] It may be thought by some that school dramatic work offers a heaven-sent
opportunity to the modernist producer who believes that " the actor should be disciplined down to the last gesture and intonation." He finds professional actors
refractory to handle. Here, surely, in the schools, is material malleable to his touch !
But the school producer is more than a producer, he is an educator. It is the boy's
self-expression he is concerned with primarily, not his own. The boy matters more
than the play.

nothing of " Hence, wilt thou lift up Olympus ? " will probably put immediate conviction into " Hence, have you taken leave of your senses ? " If one paraphrase does not have the desired effect, invent another. As soon as the actor shows comprehension, return to the text. Still more useful is the phrase which, spoken by the player under the breath, brings out the meaning of an obscure or ambiguous speech. To take a famous example of ambiguity from *Macbeth* : Lady Macbeth's " We fail," in response to her husband's " If we should fail ? " can be taken in three ways.

1. Philosophically. " We fail." *And that's that !*
2. Derisively. " We fail." *What rubbish ! Heavens, man, pull yourself together !*
3. Incredulously. " *We* fail." *Macbeth and Lady Macbeth fail ? The Macbeth who conquered Sweno fail ?*

The phrases in italics provide what has aptly been called " an emotional context " to the spoken words. To take a further example, the words " Go on " may be interpreted : (1) " Go on." *I'll follow in a moment.* (2) " Go on." *Ignore the interruption.* (3) " Go on." *Get a move on, can't you ?* (4) " Go on." *You're pulling my leg !* It is not suggested that all these variants would arise in the one context, but the *sotto voce* phrase may be illuminating even where there is no actual ambiguity. The idea is applicable to longer sentences —*e.g.* " What news shall we hear ? " *I feel so excited, don't you ?* " What news shall *we* hear ? " *No one's likely to tell us anything.*

Help from the Other Elements in Production.—It is the fundamental thesis of this book that the effective presentation of a play depends on something more than acting, however good—that it involves the creation of a new entity, a new work of art, which is the product of many contributory arts perfectly fused, making the drama " live for its audience at its highest possible emotional intensity." And not only for the audience ! Lighting and costume and setting are part of the experience of the play for the actors as well, and create an atmosphere in which their characterizations take on a fuller life. Boys playing in $X = O$ have told me that the play " suddenly became real " for them at the lighting rehearsal. In other words, they were helped to approach the play in the right mood. The blue mist from the overheads helped the beauty of the summer night to " move to miraculous birth at their imagining." This indeed seems to be the common experience of boy actors. Some of them say that costume helps even more (" I can't feel I'm really a Trojan looking at the Greek tents when I'm wearing flannel bags and looking at the Honours board "), but the general view is that costume is important chiefly in farcical, burlesque, and comic parts (which depend on a sense of the ridiculous), and that in serious plays lighting, more than any other factor, in the final stages helps to put the actor inside the skin of his part. It is not that the actor sees lighting in quite the same way as the audience ; obviously he sees more of the " works "), but the intensity and colour of the illumination bring him (perhaps even more than the audience) into subconscious harmony with the " mood " of the scene.

Clearly, there should be several rehearsals with full lighting (and costume too, if that be possible) before the " dress " rehearsal. The dress rehearsal should be a formality, not an ordeal.

6. Two Special Cases : (1) Shakespeare

" What do you do with a play of Shakespeare ? "
" Act it," I replied.   " What else can you do with a play ? "
CALDWELL COOK.

" Here is a series of memoranda of lines to be spoken by certain
actors who belonged to Shakespeare's company. The speaker is indicated in each case, and from time to time there is a reminder to the
stage-manager to have trumpets sounded or cannon discharged behind
the scenes.   There is no direct description of the appearance of the
persons, their age, their dress, their idiosyncrasies, the gesture which
accompanies the speeches, the position of the persons on stage, the
mood of a speech, nor the mood in which it is received. A character
may be calm, or may be sobbing convulsively without any direct indication in the text.   All of this by-play, without which the spoken words
are mere fragments, are gone with Burbage and Kemp, and Hemyng
and Condell, and the others who first made the plays live.   And still
we persist in putting a Shakespeare play before a child as if it were a
novel, and expect him to appreciate it.   Almost as well give him a
conductor's score of Beethoven's Ninth Symphony and expect him to
realize the splendours of the composition."

ROY MITCHELL, *Shakespeare for Community Players*, pages 2, 3.

The Problem of Length.—Numerous references to the
specific problems of Shakespearean production have already
been made, notably in the sections on " Cutting " (Chapter II.,
page 29), " Stage Business " (Chapter II., pages 36, 37), and
" Entrances " (Chapter II., page 44). The difficulty often
arises of the excessive length of time taken to perform a
complete play. This is usually due (*a*) to " dragging " of the
lines. We have urged deliberation, but with verse this can be
carried too far. (" Speak the speech, I pray you . . . trip-
pingly on the tongue ") ; (*b*) to waits between the scenes.
Shakespeare's plays must be played as they were upon his own
stage, with one scene succeeding another in a continuous flow
of action. It is fatal if there have to be pauses for scene-
changing, even if they last no more than a minute or two.

(There are forty scenes in *Antony and Cleopatra* !) Therefore, unless a setting can be devised that, with lighting changes, will provide an appropriate background for the whole of the action, it is necessary to avail oneself of some form of traverse curtain (see page 71), and play scenes more or less alternately on the unlocalized fore-stage and on the main-stage. As the players leave the fore-stage the traverse should be opened and the play proceed without pause. (Or a scene can be " faded out " by a dimming of the lights, and then, the curtains having been opened and any unwanted " props " removed, the new scene " faded in " ; but this is not so easy, electrically, as it sounds.) Sometimes the rear-stage can be divided into two with a curtain covering each portion, and sometimes curtains can be run diagonally from the centre back to the corners of the proscenium opening, allowing four different playing areas; but such devices are seldom necessary, for only a few of the scenes need any very definite indication of locality. Shakespeare's drama, says Granville-Barker, " is attached solely to its actors and their acting. . . . They carry time and place with them as they move."

Intervals.—The aim should be to render unnecessary any " re-arrangement " or telescoping of scenes. Incidentally, the division into Acts and Scenes should be ignored—you don't find it in the Quartos, and only in certain plays in the First Folio ; it is quite meaningless, and Shakespeare never bothered his head about such a thing. One or two intervals, carefully chosen, will suffice.

Other Matters.—At all times the producer should consult the original text. Most of the familiar scene directions, as well as the stage directions, are editorial accretions.

Is it necessary to add that " traditional " business should not be perpetrated automatically, but considered strictly on its merits ?

For the arrangement of " playlets " from the plays, and

for lists of musical settings to songs, see the book of Roy
Mitchell.   An orchestra for incidental music is best concealed
behind the scenes, not placed in front.

(2) *Savoy Opera*

Many schools perform " Gilbert and Sullivan " ; a word
on the subject may therefore be in season.   The writer, fervent
admirer of the operas as he was, first approached the task
of producing one of them in school without much enthusiasm ;
he was not convinced of the educational value of the venture.
He has been—almost—converted.   Certainly, if its intrinsic
cultural value be slight, and its histrionic demands not very
exacting, no other kind of work demands such a sustained
corporate effort on the part of pupils and staff.[1]

The producer should strive for originality and not for a
slavish reproduction of D'Oyly Carte " business," though he
should be warned that the almost religious fanaticism of Gilbert
and Sullivan audiences, and the well-meaning attempts of his
actors to model themselves on their professional prototypes,
will make his task difficult.   And let him never forget that
the works were intended as burlesques, not oratorios.   The
actions of D'Oyly Carte, without their spirit, may be disas-
trous.

Smooth working between the producer and the musical
director (where the two officials are not the same person) is
essential.   The music should be thoroughly known before
floor-work is attempted.   If possible, the services of the same
accompanist should be used throughout all rehearsals.   The
singing is bound to fall away when the minds of the players are
first concentrating on their movements, but once these are
satisfactory, the musical director should be called in again, and

---

[1] The co-operation of staff is a vocal necessity.

occasional action-rehearsals should be regarded as primarily " his show."

Preparation.—The production will demand exceedingly full and thorough preparation, and rigid control over every step

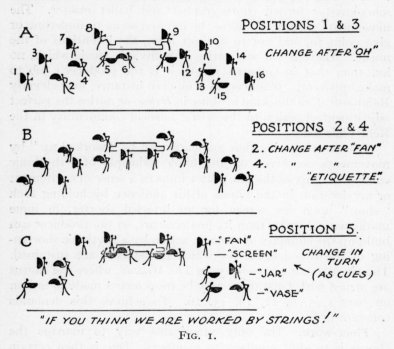

MIKADO — MEN'S CHORUS —"*GENTLEMEN OF JAPAN.*"

A

POSITIONS 1 & 3

CHANGE AFTER "OH"

B

POSITIONS 2 & 4

2. *CHANGE AFTER "FAN"*
4.   "   "   "*ETIQUETTE*"

C

POSITION 5.

—"FAN"
—"SCREEN"
—"JAR"
—"VASE"

CHANGE IN TURN (AS CUES)

"*IF YOU THINK WE ARE WORKED BY STRINGS!*"

FIG. I.

and gesture of every player from the first bar to the last. Before the producer can take his first floor-rehearsal of a chorus number lasting, say, five minutes, he will need to have spent perhaps as many hours with score and records carefully adjusting every movement to the music, not to mention the sundry minutes he will spend in the privacy of bedroom or bathroom devising dance steps. Not only will his interleaved copies of the score and libretto be covered with hieroglyphics of diagrammatized groupings, postures, gestures, and move-ments, but these hieroglyphics will themselves be the out-come of long experiment with pastel or brush. It is a case of schoolmaster turned choreographer and ballet master. The movements should, of course, be devised so as to underline or give point to, and not to distract from, the intentions of the music. There is wit and satire in Sullivan's music which, no less than that in Gilbert's words, it is the producer's job to make apparent. (Observe, as a modern instance, how cleverly Reinhardt does this kind of thing in *Helen*, or notice the perfect adjustment of action to the satiric musical commentary in the René Clair films.)

It is worth noting that audiences can be " worked up " by movements conceived on the filmic principle of " rhythmic cutting." Just as the film editor induces a sense of excitement or acceleration in the minds of his audience by holding each " shot " upon the screen for an interval shorter, in some mathematical ratio, than its predecessors, so the producer can build up the climaxes of operatic action by a rhythmic shorten-ing of the time-lengths for which movements are sustained. Thus in a 16-bar phrase (say, in *The Mikado*, where the chorus are armed with fans) there may be movements made in unison on bars 1, 5, 9, 11, 13, 15, 16. To achieve this demands constant drill.

Floor-work.—The only practicable way to manage the chorus is to allot numbers to members. One is then certain that the same individuals are in the same places at each rehearsal, and the positions can be worked out in terms of numbers. (Incidentally, when your cast is composed partly of boys and partly of masters, it may be much less embarrassing to say that " Number 15 is moving on the wrong beat " than

PLATE VI.—*She Stoops to Conquer.*

A school production by John Hampden—an example of an appropriate realistic setting, made by boys in the school workshop from the producer's scale-drawings.

The garden scene was played in front of a dark green traverse curtain, lit only by a small " flood " (from the front) with a steel-blue gelatine. The inn scene was played in an inset—rough " walls " the backs of old canvas scenery, which were rolled on stout battens behind the scenes when not in use, because lack of head-room made it impossible to " fly " them, and hauled up into place on spring-hooks lowered from the roof for the setting.

All the other scenes were played in the set which is shown in part above, and which was convincingly constructed (in sections) of thin three-ply on frames. The leaded window, with " hollyhocks " just outside, looked on to a " sky " of taut blue casement-cloth. Unfortunately the above is reproduced from a flash-light photograph.

Lighting was simple and naturalistic, dimmers being used only for the sunset and the lighting of the candles, and was softened by a free admixture of coloured light. Equipment and switchboard, all home-made, were under the stage, with the chief electrician seated so that his eyes were just above stage-level, centre front—a position of great advantage except when he made faces at the players.

BARS	Nos 11-16		Nos 1-8
10.	ASSUME POSITIONS		INTRO.
16. A.	Girls / Men	TWICE EACH WAY	Girls / Men — "DANCE A CACHUCHA"
16. B.	M G	TWICE EACH WAY.	G M — "TO THE PRETTY PITTER"
16. C.		4 KICKS EACH WAY.	"OLD XERES"
2.	WHIRL		
16. A.		TWICE EACH WAY.	"DANCE A CACHUCHA"
2.	PAUSE.		
16. B		4 KICKS EACH WAY.	"OLD XERES"
8.	PAUSE.		5½ BARS — "DANCES" 2½ " - ASSUME POSITIONS
16. A.		TWICE EACH WAY.	FINALE.
16. B.	M G	TWICE EACH WAY.	G M. "
7.	EXIT 6 — COUPLES 16,15,14. EXIT 5 COUPLES 13,12,11 4 COUPLES 10,9.		EXIT 1 — COUPLES 1,2,3. 2 COUPLES 4,5,6. 3 COUPLES 7,8.

FIG. 2.

to make the same complaint about Mr. Jones !)   Personally,
I have found it well worth the trouble to prepare large-scale
diagrams of stage positions at difficult points in the action,
and to place these on Dramatic Society and Staff Room notice-
boards (Figs. 1 and 2).   The use of a blackboard in demonstrating chorus movements is not to be despised, and I can
remember one occasion when a length of string and two
drawing-pins made immediately apparent a movement I had
despaired of teaching by oral explanation.

Slick, mechanical chorus work is only called for, of course,
in operas of a burlesque type.   In serious opera there must be
individual acting—but very restrained—by the chorus members.

The placing of the orchestra for opera may occasion some
trouble.   The ideal place is the usual place—below the stage
in front.   When the stage is very shallow in height, and there
is no orchestra pit, the only thing to do is to put the orchestra
to the side, or split it—half on each side.   The conductor, of
course, must be visible to the singers as well as the instrumentalists.

Care must, in any case, be taken to shield the orchestra
lights so that they do not distract the attention of the audience.
In the absence of specially designed lamps, 40-watt bulbs can
be used concealed in cocoa tins in which a narrow light-slit
has been cut.   The tins should be stoved black and fixed to the
music stands with swivel brackets.   But the tins get very hot,
and you may find it better to use 12-watt bulbs such as are
used on motor-cars.

CHAPTER III.—THE PERMANENT SETTING

" PERMANENT " may seem an inapt term to apply to something which is perhaps erected for only a few weeks in the year. By it is meant the general structural framework within which the specific scenery for various productions can be fitted. If the general framework is on sound lines the problem of " setting " is enormously facilitated.

The Platform.—The basis is the stage platform itself. For those who are in the fortunate position of being able to control the actual construction of their platform, a whole host of fascinating problems are opened up. Should it be of one level or built up of different planes with the fore-stage descending in steps to the auditorium ? Should the fore-stage project beyond the proscenium arch ? Indeed, should there be a proscenium arch at all ? The curious reader is recommended to consult the chapter on " Theatre Design " in Harold Ridge's book on *Stage Lighting*, where there is a debate between Ridge and Terence Gray on the proscenium controversy. He would also do well to look (with a discriminating eye) at Wilson's *Small Stage and its Equipment*. (I, personally, regard the stage walls of his " all-purposes " stage as likely to be a thundering nuisance.) Ridge speaks highly of Roy Mitchell's *School Theatre*. This book is out of print, and I have been unable to consult a copy, but I understand that he advocates some variant of the Copeau stage, which implies an architectural structure with a variety of acting levels. (Sheldon Cheney; page 115, Plates XCVII., XCVIII.). It is my view that the future of the theatre lies with sculptured stages (without proscenium) of this kind ; for Shakespearean and classical plays they are ideal, but so far as schools are concerned they do not seem to me to be very feasible. A fore-stage descending in steps means a big encroachment into the auditorium—for steps, to be of any practical use, must be at least twice as wide as they are high ; a fore-stage projecting beyond the proscenium arch is difficult to light (it necessitates spotlights in the roof or gallery) ; and the abolition of the proscenium involves technical problems (particularly of lighting) which, in schools at any rate, are wellnigh insoluble.

In any case, most school producers have to work with the platform they happen to have—a plain rectangular structure or dais, let us assume, at one end of the school hall. On that basis what can we achieve ?

Where such a platform does not extend across the whole width of the hall, the first desirable thing is to build an extension either side so that it does. It is an intolerable nuisance if the actors have to clamber up steps every time they enter the stage from the wings, and it greatly complicates the setting and moving of scenery. The side portions of the stage are quite as important as the acting area. The extension (like the stage itself) should be a firm, non-creaking affair, with the planking (running from back to front) screwed to the trestles, and the trestles screwed to the floor. It may well include one or two " plug sockets " or traps for lighting connections.

Access to this extended stage from the dressing-rooms will depend, naturally, on the disposition of doors in the particular hall. Steps from door to stage level may have to be let in to the extensions (as in Figs. 4 and 5). If there is not a door for entrance available either side (and again, in those tragic cases where there is *no* door and the whole cast has to wait in the wings all the evening), it will be necessary to arrange a passage-way at the back of the stage. This may be behind the back-cloth, or, better still, it may be possible to bring the platform forward a few feet from the back wall, leaving a passage-way at floor-level. Such a gap has advantages in any case, as it provides a pit into which the back-cloth can be allowed to hang. Ground lighting of the cloth, which otherwise (in the absence of a special trough sunk in the platform) demands the building up of some scenic structure on the stage to hide the lights, is greatly simplified. A passage-way behind a back-cloth should never be used if a route behind the hall is available ; there is the double risk of noise and of some one knocking the cloth and sending a palpable shudder through the " sky."

The Proscenium Frame.—Given the platform, the necessity arises to screen such parts of it as it is inadvisable for the audience to see, and also, at times, to screen off the acting area itself, for the purpose of changing scenery. In the real theatre the stage is separated from the auditorium by the proscenium wall, behind which moves the front curtain. In the school theatre such a proscenium is best constructed of draperies, a pelmet and side pieces being hung in pleats from the roof or from a cross beam. (Fig. 4 will suggest a method of economizing a few feet of side curtain, though at the risk of sway, unless it is held to the roof by wooden laths instead of ropes, as shown.) In the writer's school the side curtains are hung on tracks, so that the front-stage opening can be extended almost to the side walls if desired. If the front curtain is of the draw type, and will extend from wall to wall, the side pieces are not strictly necessary.

The depth of the pelmet must be determined by experiment —either on the spot or with the aid of scale drawings (side elevations) of hall and stage. The higher the stage opening— within limits—the greater the possibility of impressive scenic effects : you cannot convey the sense of tragedy through a squat frame. On the other hand, the greater the difficulty of masking the overhead works. The pelmet should certainly be high enough above the stage to afford people in the balcony (if there is one) a full view of the whole acting area—and in this connection it must be remembered that figures at the back of the stage are often grouped on steps or elevations.

The " False Proscenium."—But it is idle to expect either the pelmet or the side pieces by themselves to provide adequate screening. Some kind of false proscenium, some distance behind the first, will be necessary. One of the chief differences between school stages and the stages of commercial theatres (even the smallest) is the distance of the players from the footlights ; on the commercial stage there are usually several non-committal black flats, or "torments," between the

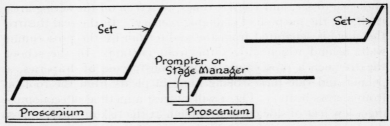

FIG. 3.—Two methods.

proscenium and the actual " set " which screen a great deal of wing space (and, incidentally, afford electrician and stage manager a view of the stage—*e.g.* Fig. 3). Some touring companies (*e.g.* The Chauve-Souris) carry their own false proscenium around with them, setting it well within the fixed proscenium.

For school purposes, where it may be desired to use even the front corners of the stage, an arrangement, as in Fig. 4, should be found adequate. Overhead, a black opaque border —" B "—(canvas preferably), hanging from a batten pulleyed to the roof or to an overhead beam, screens the upper works and back lights. This border (unlike the pelmet itself) can be very easily adjusted. It should obviate the necessity for any hideous " sky-borders " behind it. If further borders are necessary, let them be frankly formal, like this one.[1] They should be dull black, so as to be unaffected by the colours of the overhead lights. They should hang with a perfectly straight and horizontal lower edge. (Borders of black velvet, pleated like the pelmet itself, are permissible with an all-black velvet drapery surround such as the Chauve-Souris use.) Our " border B," which was at first merely a length of dyed calico (and barely opaque!), is now a properly made wood-and-canvas framework (two " flats," 15 feet by 6 feet each, hinged end to end, a strip of black velvet making the hinge light-tight). By varying the angle at which the two black wing flats stand, and by moving the pulleys overhead which hold " border B " (our pulleys are *tied* to beams running back to front, and the lashings can be slid along), it is possible to adjust the distance of this false proscenium behind the real one. If you want your actors to occupy the very front part of the stage you must hang some lights between this border and the pelmet ; otherwise it is best to keep all the lighting behind the border, and to play more up stage.

Within this frame the setting, whether of draperies or flats, is arranged.

The Traverse Curtain.—For school purposes a traverse curtain to shut off the front portion of the stage is highly desirable. For classical drama it is far more important than the front curtain. Scenes can be played alternately on front stage and full stage, the fore-stage being non-localized, and changes of scenery being made meanwhile behind the traverse. Jacobean dramatists, at a time when the inner stage of the Elizabethan theatre was being localized by the use of simple properties, seem to have " worked " the alternation idea

---

[1] With " straight " interior sets further borders should never be used ; a ceiling piece should be made.

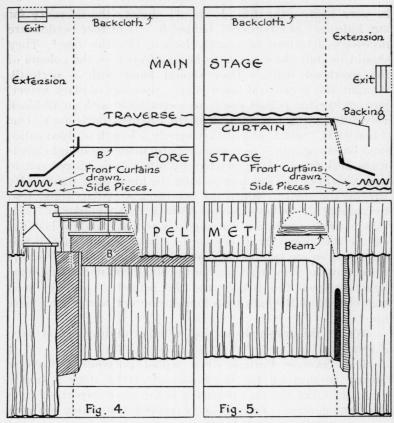

Two possible arrangements showing plan and elevation.

deliberately.   Many eighteenth-century plays (Sheridan's *St. Patrick's Day*, for instance) fit the theory like a glove.   Shakespeare can best be produced in terms of it.

Fore-stage Portals.—For schools doing exclusively this kind of work, it may be advisable to formalize the fore-stage by an architectural unit, such as the side portal in Fig. 4, which can stand throughout the show, or indeed many shows. Commenting on the use of portals of this kind, Cheney says : " The advantage is not only in the elimination of disillusioning waits between the scenes, but in the audience's sense of being always in the theatre, at the same theatre—as against the old system where the scenic designer spent his talent trying to give the spectator an illusion of being away from a stage and in a succession of real places. (A difficult distinction, but at the very heart of modernist theories of the theatre.) The standing portals also afford a sub-conscious feeling of holding together the action, of continuity, of oneness, a sort of continuous physical accompaniment that has its tying-together effect like the accompaniment of appropriate light or music. In the last analysis this is a method of formalizing or conventionalizing the front portion of the stage while keeping the up-stage space free for more or less realistic manipulation." [1]

An arrangement of this kind is particularly appropriate to the Comedy of Manners ; indeed, it derives from a feature of the Restoration theatres. Applied to an isolated play, its consideration really belongs to the next chapter. The question here is whether it should form part of the " permanent setting."

The portal shown in Fig. 5 would be best contained in a 4-foot flat held between two fixed pillars of substantial timber ; any other 4-foot unit could then be clamped in its place in a few seconds.

The traverse curtain itself can be suspended from a structure built on stage as part of this formalized front set (as in Fig. 5), instead of from the roof or a batten (as in Fig. 4). Where no assistance can be obtained from the roof, and the frame has to be built up instead of being hung, a structure of this kind, substantial enough to carry lighting units as well as the

---

[1] *Stage Decoration*, page 69.

traverse, is unavoidable. Being heavy and difficult to erect, it would require to stand permanently. It would lack the merit of flexibility, and would limit the range of plays which could be performed.

Where such a structure is erected the false proscenium will be unnecessary.

The Proscenium Curtain : Methods of Moving.—Behind the proscenium frame moves the proscenium curtain.

There are three ways of " opening " a curtain : (*a*) " Flying "—*i.e.* hauling it straight up. Feasible in halls with high

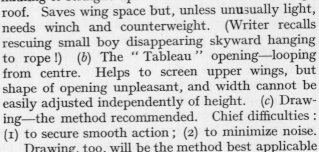

roof. Saves wing space but, unless unusually light, needs winch and counterweight. (Writer recalls rescuing small boy disappearing skyward hanging to rope !) (*b*) The " Tableau " opening—looping from centre. Helps to screen upper wings, but shape of opening unpleasant, and width cannot be easily adjusted independently of height. (*c*) Drawing—the method recommended. Chief difficulties : (1) to secure smooth action ; (2) to minimize noise. Drawing, too, will be the method best applicable to the traverse curtain.

FIG. 6.

Fixed Tracks.—If possible, the curtains should move on fixed tracks. Those employed for domestic curtains will be found too frail for the heavier stage curtains, though you can get (for 1s. a foot) a strong track in brass with steel fittings that will carry all but velvet. The best known tracks for theatrical curtains are those made by the Hall Manufacturing Company, Lambeth, whose valuable catalogue should be consulted. Their 30-foot two-part track for medium weight curtains costs £8, 15s. The simplest tracks which the writer has seen are those used by the Chauve-Souris Company ; they consist of slotted steel tubes, along which slide spherical wooden bobbins (see Fig. 6). The bobbins can be purchased, and possibly the tracks could be imitated in hard wood.

Alternatives to Tracks.—Alternatively the curtains can be hung on rings running on a metal pipe. (Noisy, but useful for short lengths and for a traverse running on a rigid built-up framework.) Another method is shown in Fig. 7, and will commend itself as the cheapest and most easily adaptable. The curtain is hung on rope wire (D) fixed (it can be knotted) to a turnscrew (B), which is attached to a coach-bolt (A) driven into an overhead beam or a batten pulleyed from the roof.

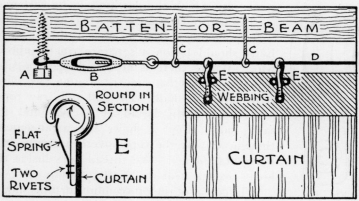

FIG. 7.

Alternatively it can be attached to a hook in a side wall. The wire is then tightened to banjo pitch by a turnscrew. With large size turnscrews a tightening of 8 inches can be effected at each end of the wire. The screw-hooks (C) check the curtain being drawn out or pulled back too far. Another form of check on the draw is by a cord attached from the wall to the last hook. This is useful when there is no overhead beam, and again when a curtain which does not extend the full width of the hall when drawn has been opened back (behind the side pieces) right to the wall.

We have had much trouble with hooks breaking or jamming, and the type illustrated (E) represents a choice born of long experiment. The spring should be of the flat type, and to minimize friction the section of hook touching the wire should be round, *not* square. These cost 3s. 6d. a dozen. At twice that cost you can obtain hard wood bobbins (Fig. 8) which run on the wires quite noiselessly, and are practically " jam-proof." (If you can dispense with the webbing attachment, 4s. a dozen.) But as these are over an inch wide they limit the space into which the curtain can be gathered.

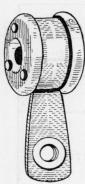

The Centre Overlap.—The two halves of the curtain should overlap a few feet in the centre. Each should be on a separate track, pipe or wire. Where there is no attachment possible to a beam this may mean running two wires right across the hall. The pull and draw ropes (clearly labelled) should be at one and the same side. Fig. 9 shows the arrangement, though actually the ropes overhead move in a horizontal plane. (We thread ours inside the hooks, except near the centre overlap.)

Fig. 8.

The colour of the proscenium curtains should be chosen with some regard for the character of the hall. The writer's choice would be for silver-grey where possible. The only really fitting material is " velvet " (which means, in such cases, furnishing velour). A set, with pelmet and side pieces, for a stage 20 feet by 40 feet, costs about £30, allowing for pleating. The plush becomes damaged by folding, and we store ours by hanging them under a dust cover in a corner of the hall. Alternative materials are discussed in the section on draperies.

The Back-cloth.—Another piece of " permanent " equipment remains to be mentioned. That is the back-cloth—a canvas sheet, theoretically wrinkleless, painted (*not* with the leafy foliage and billowing, if static, clouds of the nineteenth century) in some even neutral colour, such as pale blue or grey, upon which the real painting can be done with light. It should be secured top and bottom (the canvas screwed between double battens), and stretched as tightly as possible. It can also be laced to upright battens either side. The back wall of the stage distempered is even better than a cloth if its surface is even. In art theatres a special curved wall of plaster is used—the cyclorama or light dome—which by its diffusion of light enables wonderful effects of distance and atmosphere to be obtained. But a canvas sheet provides ample scope for magic. It extends the range of the producer a hundredfold, both in choice of plays and treatment. For " outdoor " scenes it is indispensable. The farther back it can be placed the better the illusion of limitless space.[1] Its height must be determined by experiment ; if it is too low you are bound to resort to borders to screen the upward gaze of people in the front seats. On a stage 17 feet deep, with a proscenium opening 12 feet high, it should be at least 20 feet high—and higher if there is no false proscenium.

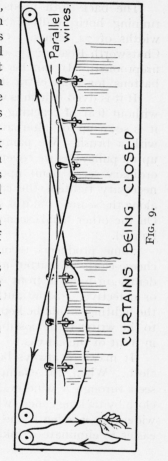

Parallel wires.

CURTAINS BEING CLOSED

Fig. 9.

[1] A *canvas* cyclorama hung in a curve is, of course, feasible if you can afford (a) the room, (b) the overhead framework.

The back-cloth needs to be well made, with the seams running horizontally. (Scene canvas is made normally in widths of 72 inches.) Our cloth was made by McDougall, Chatsworth Road, E.15, and cost £4, 7s. 6d. (30 feet by 20 feet, fireproofed). It can be webbed and taped, for *tying* to the battens, for a few extra shillings.

If it is dyed (which is what is recommended) it can be rolled without fear of cracking. The dyeing should be done before it is sewn up, or, alternatively, analine dye can be painted on with a brush. We painted ours with Walpamur, hauling it up on pulleys as we covered it. The main objections to using ordinary scene paint upon it are: (*a*) the priming which is necessary tightens the canvas and tends to make it wrinkle along the seams ; (*b*) it is difficult to avoid leaving brush marks. On the other hand, scene paint appears more luminous when lighted.

Some producers recommend a gauze cyclorama of dyed cheese-cloth or butter muslin.[1] This can be used independently, or hung in front of a canvas back-cloth that is wrinkled or defective. (Some authorities urge that in the latter case the lighting should be kept off the gauze, but this does not seem to the writer to be possible ; he would use it only a few inches in front of the canvas.)

It may not always be convenient to use so large a back-cloth. When, for example, all that is needed is a skyscape seen through a window, it may be better to make a special cloth by tacking calico (which can be obtained up to 100 inches wide) to a wooden frame, keeping it stretched tight. It is far easier to eliminate wrinkles on a small cloth such as this, and

---

[1] Theatrical gauze will be found too " open " for this purpose, though it is capable of astounding effects if properly lit. Stretched tight on a frame and lit obliquely from behind by lights concealed from the audience, it assumes a kind of opaque radiance—a mist of light that conveniently screens what lies beyond—*e.g.* the Chauve-Souris item of " The Hairdresser's Shop Window ! " It is cheap, too—4s. a yard (9 *yards* wide).

it need not be painted. Plate XI. illustrates the use of special cloths of this kind.

The Roof.—The roof is as important to the scenic manager as the stage floor is to the actor. In the professional theatre, of course, there is a grid high up above the stage containing the pulleys over which run the various sets of lines holding the battens for draperies, drop-scenes, or lights. The batten is usually supported at each end and at the middle, and the ropes are arranged so that they can be taken together to a cleat placed in the wings or on a special platform. (see Fig. 10). (A counter-weight system enables even the heaviest batten-loads

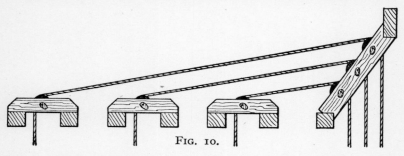

FIG. 10.

to be pulleyed by hand.) Fortunately most school halls have beams overhead to which pulleys can be fixed ; and supplementary or cross beams of, say, 4-inch by 4-inch redwood may be lashed across them at convenient intervals. If it is impossible to get a purchase on the roof in this way, pulleys may be fixed near the roof in the side walls, and the batten hauled up by means of a rope at each end of it. (Indeed, single-pull haulage may be a luxury if you *have* got beams overhead, and the centre rope will not be necessary unless the battens are long (or thin) enough to sag. Our battens are all made of 2-inch by 4-inch timber,[1] bought in 24-foot lengths, and used

[1] " Did I say all ? " Our batten for the proscenium spotlights is a length of iron piping.

with the 4-inch face vertical. When necessary two of these lengths are joined by means of a central overlap, secured with three bolts. For pulleys which are not permanently fixed, but merely lashed, we use tie-up pulleys, costing 4d. each single, 6d. double.

PLATE VII.—Scene from the Centenary Review " Let us be Tolerant "
at University College School.

Amusing example of formalism, with use of coloured cardboard
profile pieces against a black surround.

CHAPTER IV.—SCENE DESIGN

" It is idle to talk about the distraction of scenery, because the question here is not how to create some distracting scenery, but rather how to create a place which harmonizes with the thoughts of the poet."

CRAIG, *The Art of the Theatre.*

" A stage is a place to act in, not a picture to act against."

CRAIG, *A Production.*

" The art of designing stage settings is the art not of making pictures, but of relating them to living presences."

LEE SIMONSON, *The Stage is Set.*

The Modern Conception of Scene Design.—Fashions in stage decoration, like other fashions, change. The changes are instructive. They illustrate the changing conceptions of the very nature of the theatre.

The perspective backgrounds—wings, borders, and drop-scenes—and the painted shadows which the nineteenth-century theatre took over from the operatic stage have gone, it may be hoped, for good. Antoine and the producers of Ibsen and other realists raised the revolt, and a veritable orgy of naturalism followed : windows acquired real ledges, book-cases real books, and much that was utterly artificial was swept away ; unfortunately a great deal that, while natural, was unnecessary was put in its place, so that the actor often became lost in a welter of bric-à-brac. Miracles of " exact " representation were achieved. Interiors were portrayed " to the life." And if the works of the house-furnisher could thus be imitated, why not those of the Almighty ? Soon, people who had never stopped for a moment to watch the beauty of a shower in the street became frantic with enthusiasm when they beheld " rain " upon the stage. This tradition dies hard. But in the better commercial theatres—of Reinhardt, say, or Cochran, or Basil Dean—the last twenty-five years have seen a continual " simplifying and making tasteful " of the realistic setting, aided especially by advances in the æsthetics of lighting. Ironically enough, the movement has derived its inspiration from men like Craig and Appia, who have them-selves never compromised with realism for an instant.

" Actuality, accuracy of detail, is useless on the stage," wrote Craig. " By means of *suggestion* you may bring on a sense of all things . . ." So depiction passed into suggestion, a single pillar and a stained-glass window came to stand for a cathedral, a tree for a forest, a " rug and a throne against a tapestry " for the king's audience hall.

" Tasteful simplification," however, implies design, and it brought the painters back to the theatre—Stern, Norman Wilkinson, Rutherston, and the rest.[1] But a stage setting differs from a painting in that it needs to be plastic, three-dimensional, " for the actor himself is in the round, and a pictorial background will always be out of consonance with his presence." Once more the cry arose " forget the picture, abandon depiction, get back to the theatre," and so we arrive at the modernists and the trend towards expressionism, towards abstraction, towards " constructivist " and " space " stages.

The designer who once viewed the stage with the eyes of an easel-painter, then with the eyes of a photographer, now sees it with the vision of the architect. But the fundamental difference between scene-design half a century ago and now is this : then, when it meant merely " painting scenery," or at its best simply " making striking stage pictures," it was

---

[1] The stylized pictorialism of Bakst and the Russian ballet, for all the influence of its gorgeous colourings, was, in a way, a thing apart. Backgrounds that would be mere distraction in ordinary drama were perfectly apt in dance-drama aiming at sensuous effect.

considered as something extraneous to the production, as
" a splendour added " ; now it is considered as an integral
part of a drama that can itself only come to fullest life through
a perfect " co-ordination of its emotional appeals." [1]

These developments contain profound lessons for those of
us who work with drama in the schools, and I cannot too
strongly urge producers to study them in the magnificent
illustrations to Sheldon Cheney's *Stage Decoration*, or Fuerst
and Hume's *Twentieth Century Stage Decoration*, or other
works listed in the Bibliography. The above paragraphs are
based very largely upon Cheney's brilliant preface.

Types of Setting.—The producer's own method of approach
will depend on the type of drama he is presenting. If he is
presenting Comedy of Manners he will need something formal
and stylized ; if he is presenting fantasy he will need to get as
far away from reality as he can.[2] Generally speaking, as the
practical Mr. Cochran has pointed out, musical comedy, revue,
ballet, give opportunities for the lavishly picturesque, " domestic comedy and naturalistic drama provide a vehicle for
neo-realistic settings, Shakespeare and classic drama generally
—and a number of modern plays—lend themselves to more
abstract scenic treatment." To which may be added the
counsel of Mr. Ridge of the Cambridge Festival Theatre—that
shining example amongst " Little " Theatres—" realism should
always be avoided unless demanded by the play. All poetic
works lose rather than gain by elaborate scenery, and gain
rather than lose by elaborate lighting. A producer should
call upon the imagination of his audience, stimulate and
use it."

---

[1] Cheney. *Cp.* Lee Simonson's definition : " The creation of plastic forms and
spaces that are an integral part of the acting of any play, and project its meaning."

[2] *Cp.* Craig's description of a model for *The Importance of Being Earnest* :
" You will see that the scene is very artificial, just as the play is artificial. This first
scene is the interior of a bachelor's apartments ; but it is more than that—it is
such an apartment seen through the temperament of Wilde."—*The Theatre Advancing*, pages 226–227.

The abstract setting has the virtue of simplicity. Yet one must beware of merely negative virtues. The setting is the background for the action. It should suggest, however tentatively, the *locale*. At the same time it should express the spirit of the play and contrive, unobtrusively, to put the spectator " in the best possible frame of mind to understand and enjoy " the action. Any kind of background will not do. As Jeffreys points out : " It would obviously be wrong to play Clemence Dane's *Granite* before curtains whose yielding folds were entirely out of keeping with the spirit of the play ; and it would be absurd to play *A Midsummer Night's Dream* before a solid block of masonry." There can be good " simple " settings, and bad ones.

The designer, as we have said, must first seek to apprehend the underlying idea of the drama. He has then to express this by his use of line and colour. A burlesque, it is evident, will ask for fantastic colours and exaggerated outlines ; excitement may be induced by sudden angles and jagged lines ; bountiful content by warm tones and piled-up curves ; dignity and even a sense of impending doom by towering vertical lines. (Of the psychological value of colour we shall have more to say when we are discussing lighting, but it is evident that all the elements in the setting—lighting, costumes, properties, as well as " scenery " in the narrow sense—must be envisaged as one.)

The Feeling of Unity.—The various scenes should contribute in feeling to the unity of the whole work. This sense of unity can be helped both by colour and by form—by colour if all the scenes are variations on some dominant hue ; by form if the scenes are built from the same units, or contain some common element. For an illustration of unity achieved by use of colour, the reader may be referred to Craig's famous visualization of scenes for *Macbeth*. (*On the Art of the Theatre*, pp. 22–26.)

Examples of the unifying influence of common form are

[*Photos by Author.*

PLATE VIII.—*The Gondoliers, Acts I. and II.*
Illustrating simple variation of units.
(*See pages* 87–88.)

found in the fore-stage portals discussed in the last chapter, in unit-system settings, and in skeleton settings.

In unit-system settings the various scenes are built entirely from interchangeable units (" flats " or screens, or three-dimensional objects; see page 94). In skeleton settings the changes of scene are effected by the alteration of minor elements in a skeleton framework—a recess for a doorway, a fireplace for a window.

Ivor Brown recently described how Strohm produced *Urfaust* in London " with only the scantiest furniture of stage-effect. The two Gothic arches of his simple setting were either filled or emptied to suggest a room or a street ; a little pivoting

FIG. 11.

to clear the stage, and a single tree beside them took us to the country. The lighting was brilliantly employed to emphasize these simple transformations, and one will not easily forget the sweet blue cleanliness that shone as bright as poet's words to give the purity of Margarethe's attic." Fig. 11 suggests variations on a skeleton set of this sort, with the main changes effected by black and silver-grey curtains. Observe the effect of height secured by the vertical lines in the " throne-room " scene.

The three illustrations from *R.U.R.* (Plates IX., X., XV.) again show variations imposed upon a skeleton framework, with changes of scene effected by the use of panels and curtains (and formalized furniture)—and, of course, by lighting. Incidentally, the office bookcase in Act I. not only hides the gap

THREE ARRANGEMENTS OF A BOX-SET, SHOWING SIGHT-LINES.

Key :

A Fireplace.	C Door.	E Back-cloth.
B Window.	D Ground-row.	F Hall.

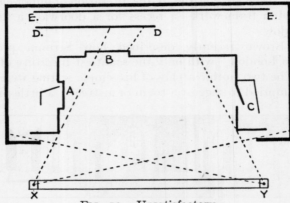

FIG. 12.—Unsatisfactory.

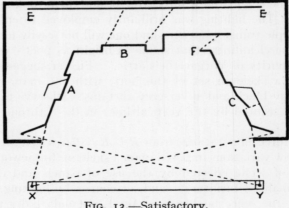

FIG. 13.—Satisfactory.

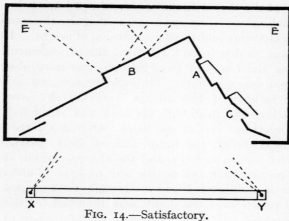

FIG. 14.—Satisfactory.

which has to accommodate the fireplace in Act II., but is so arranged that its larger books pass beyond the plane of the wall into the gap, giving the desired illusion of modernist " built-in " furniture.

A great advantage of a skeleton setting is that the basic framework, which is permanent, can be built with great rigidity. In this case the main beams were bracketed securely to the floor, and carried up and lashed to the hall beams overhead, so that doors on the set could be banged to with impunity, and thirty Robots could swarm over the terrace at the back without causing a tremor.

The two settings for *The Gondoliers* (Plate VIII.) illustrate the same principle and, incidentally, show how advantage may sometimes be taken of the natural features of some particular stage. On the back wall of the school hall in question there projects an ornamental balcony. Normally, the back-cloth had to be dropped in front of this, so that three or four feet of valuable stage depth are wasted. The *Gondoliers* settings were designed to overcome this difficulty. The satin hangings of the throne in Act 2 were draped upon the balcony itself, black velvet being employed to disguise the squat underside of the balcony and to give an illusion of height.   The whole of this was hidden in Act 1 behind the arrangement of flats containing the fountain piece (which, you may observe, fits into an old doorway flat).   Through the recessed alcoves was seen the fathomless blue of the Venetian sky—two special frame back-cloths, flush with the back wall of the hall, powerfully lit overhead and at the base.   After Act 1 the fountain piece was removed, the lights cleared away, black curtains pulled over the back-cloths, and the alcoves—minus their base panels—pushed back against the wall to serve as arches.   The side-flats seen in Act I. stood through both scenes, except that the panels over the doors were removed for the second. All the scenery had been stippled in the first place to suggest the texture of stone-work, and then spattered on the broken-colour principle described in a later chapter, so that it was possible, by variations of lighting, to change its basic tone completely between the acts.

Scale Drawings and Sight-lines.—Having made sketches of the scenes he requires, the producer or designer should prepare ground-plans to scale, showing exactly where the various units are to be fitted on the stage.   Similarly, designs for furniture must take the practical form of scale drawings.

Sight-lines should be drawn on the ground-plan of the settings to test whether all members of the audience will receive a clear view.   In Fig. 12 the spectator X misses the fireplace, and the spectator Y misses the doorway, and the proscenium masking is unsatisfactory.   Figs. 13 and 14 show better arrangements.   (See also Fig. 22, page 108.)

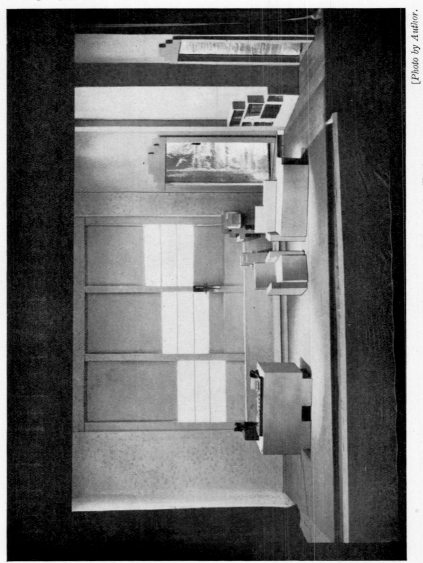

PLATE IX.—*R.U.R.*, *Act I.*—The Central Office of the Factory, A.D. 1950.

[*Photo by Author.*]

[Photo by Author.

Backing on page 89.

PLATE X.—*R.U.R., Act III.*—Helena's Drawing-room.

" Are we to sell—or destroy ? "

Plates IX., X., and XV. illustrate variation of units on a skeleton frame.

(*See pages 85–87.*)

CHAPTER V.—THE ELEMENTS OF THE SETTING

" Scenery " may be taken to consist of (*a*) draperies ; (*b*) painted units—(1) canvas-covered frames (called " flats ") and screens, (2) three-dimensional pieces such as pillars, steps, platforms, door-frames, windows, etc., (3) cut-out " profile " pieces ; (*c*) furniture.

Drop-scenes can be ignored as obsolete.

Draperies.—Drapery curtains will often be the school producer's best friend. Their rich folds and their susceptibilities to the beauties of light afford magnificent opportunities to any one who can use line and mass with purpose and effect. They are especially valuable for formal and abstract settings. But in modern scenes, door and window units, braced from the back, can be fitted into the curtain surround, shorter lengths of curtain being hung above or below them. One of the most effective drawing-room sets I have ever seen on any stage consisted of a black velvet surround, with the door-frames, windows, and the modernist furniture picked out in delicate pale blue-mauve.

A complete back-surround of curtains can be hung on a framework of battens (assembled on the stage floor and pulleyed up to hang just below the light-battens). A framework of rope-wire is possible if there is a rigid proscenium to take the back-to-front attachment, but is less flexible, and may hinder the hauling up of light-battens and borders. This last consideration applies to the endless track which is sometimes recommended to facilitate the reversal of curtains which are backed in another colour. Such difficulties are avoided in the

admirable system recommended by Mr. Ridge, which I venture
to adapt in Fig. 15.

The vice of the curtain-surround is that it encourages
laziness. To use it without variation throughout a play will
not induce in the audience (as settings should) the various
moods appropriate to different scenes. Mr. Ernest Milton's
jibes at the " meagre accoutrements of the curtain and tomb-
stone school " are not entirely misplaced.

The most useful colours for drapery-curtains are black and

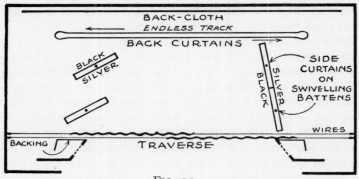

FIG. 15.

silver-grey, or fawn. If only one set is possible, the usual
advice is to avoid black because it absorbs so much light.
On the other hand, so many things can be done with black
curtains that are impossible with other colours that no company can consider itself properly equipped until it possesses a
set. This absorption of light makes it possible, even on a
small platform, to employ the convention of the " space
stage " (see page 103), and the fact that shadows are not
apparent on the black makes it possible to throw stronger light
on the characters than would otherwise be possible. (There is
no trouble with " multiple shadows " from footlights.) Black

often makes the most suitable background to brilliant colour.[1] Normally it kills the third dimension (see Plate VII.), though in a play such as *The Discovery* it can be used, as Mr. Hampden suggests, to convey the immensity of night. But perhaps a company whose means of illumination are more " general " than " specific " would be advised not to make black its first choice.

As for materials,[2] velour is expensive and heavy, but has the essential quality of opaqueness, and hangs better than anything else. Bolton sheeting is the best substitute ; it hangs well, dyes well, and is reasonably thick. Casement cloth shows a considerable amount of light through, but can be backed in another colour. (Its surface is too shiny for it to be satisfactory in black.) If you are doing revue work, it is useful to have a set of curtains that can " take " coloured light ; silver-grey is best for this in velour or Bolton sheeting, but nothing beats a satin of a very pale purple shade—it can be turned any colour.[3] Satin, of course, is very expensive ; cheaper substitutes—sateen, or artificial silk—will not have enough " body " to give good service, but can be backed on to some other material. " Silk slub rep " is quite pleasing ; the Community Drama League have sets of black velour curtains backed with it in various shades. (Made by Alfred Brookes, 6 Church Street, Clapham. This firm will make a set of these reversible draperies—48 feet long in eight sections, with an 18-foot drop—for £28. Velour, backed with fireproofed case-

---

[1] For example, the Chauve-Souris, whose scenes are full of colour, play in a setting of black velour (with two traverses !).

[2] The choice may be limited by the fire regulations of the local authority. The London County Council insist that materials must be fireproof in their nature, and not merely fireproofed.

[3] (A footnote for the opulent only.) Waring and Gillows supply a beautiful satin of this shade (Sample No. 20232, " as used for the Paramount Theatre, Leeds "). We have found the lighting effects possible upon it so beautiful and striking as to yield, almost unaided, one of our most successful Revue "numbers." The same firm recommend goathair damask, which not only satisfies the London County Council's requirements, but has an exceedingly fine surface, with a high sheen which reflects light admirably.

ment, £22, 10s. Casement both sides, £12.) To the average school one would recommend this programme : first, draperies and traverse in grey Bolton sheeting ; second, draperies in black velour ; third, sateen or slub rep backed on to the Bolton sheeting draperies.

Draperies are best made in sections of 6 or 8 feet ; the sections can be used separately, or as wing pieces, or continuously end to end ; you can even join them up with press studs. With two sets of them you can get varied effects— *e.g.* black and grey panels alternating, or the grey draped or bunched in front to show an edging of black. The proscenium (and perhaps the traverse) curtains are best pleated at the head to allow for fullness ; this takes a half or a third as much material again. For the drapery curtains this pleating is not essential ; fullness can be regulated by the closeness together of the hooks or bobbins. All curtains should be weighted at the bottom with bags of lead shot, or by a chain sewn in the hem. (A chain has the advantage that it does not burst.)

The making of stage curtains is an expert job. It is false economy to attempt to do it yourself, or to have it done by a small firm.

"**Flats.**"—Ordinary scenes—*e.g.* of rooms—in the theatre are built up of various "flats" lashed together. The usual width of a flat is 5 feet 9 inches (Fig. 19), but for small stages I would recommend 4 feet as more suitable, and also as easier to move. Bigger flats (*e.g.* to take archways) or smaller ones (*e.g.* "jogs" for recesses in walls—most useful) should be in terms of the unit—twice or thrice or half its size. Door and window pieces are clamped into the frames. For example, into D in Fig. 16 could be fitted a French window (with black tape for the lattice), a folding door, a great Tudor chimney-piece, or simply a curtain. Endless changes can be rung on a set of these units.

When such flats are used as part of the conventional

[*Photo by Author.*

PLATE XI.—Screen setting for *The Mikado, Act I.*
(*See page 95.*)

" box-set," they need to be somewhat taller than the proscenium opening (say 15 feet, with a 12-foot opening). But, given a background of black curtains and some spotlights, much can be done with 8-foot or 10-foot flats. Two or three of them can be placed on stage, without either ceiling or lateral continuation, " like bits of reality floating in space," to give mere indication of locality, mere suggestion of place—a corner of a room, a section of an office wall. Readers may remember the " dentist's surgery " in the Chauve-Souris programme as an example—one of the few seen on professional stages in this

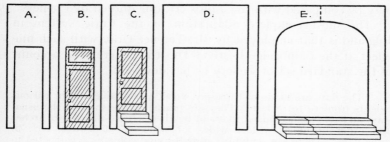

FIG. 16.—Illustrating the unit principle.

country. There are some interesting illustrations given by Cheney (Plates CXV., CXXVII.).

Screens.—Screens, as the term is most often used in treatises on the theatre, are really flats painted in monochrome and employed in a formal or non-representational way. Cheney says of them : " They have the curtain's advantages of providing a simple and neutral background, emphasizing the actor, and offering abstract decorative possibilities ; and they are more adaptable, can be arranged in endless combinations, with extraordinary different emotional suggestion." The most famous system of screens is that invented by Craig, the only practical account of which known to the writer is that quoted by Cheney from a number of *The Mask*. " Through its use," Craig claimed, " we obtain a sense of harmony and a sense of variety at the same time. We may be said to have recovered one of the unities of the Greek drama without losing any of the variety of the Shakespearean drama." Craig intended his screens to be in continuous motion, so that one scene passed into another without any break. Those interested in the subject should read Stanislavsky's account of Craig's use of screens in his production of *Hamlet* at Moscow, probably one of the most exciting accounts of a production ever written, and a most illuminating sidelight on *Hamlet*. The passage may be compared with the *Times* critique quoted by Cheney.

The most complete adaptation of the Craig system in England is that employed by Mr. Terence Gray with such fine effect at the Cambridge Festival Theatre. Here is an account of the standard set of scenery he has devised :

" The flats are made of three-ply wood, 4 feet wide and in various heights from 10 to 18 feet. They are braced to the stage in the usual way, and sometimes hinged to stand by themselves. There are arches and other openings, 3 feet wide, for windows, doorways, etc., in some flats. There are a number of half-round columns constructed in the same way as the flats, and of the same heights. There are boxes 18 inches square and in two lengths, 3 and 4 feet, covered with floor board on one side and at the ends, to enable them to be stood upon, and three-ply on the other side ; one side is left open. There are sets of steps of the same widths and heights, semicircular, triangular, and rectangular. The boxes can be built up one upon another together with the steps, and can be fitted into the openings with the flats. An almost infinite variety of scenes can thus be made. The flats and boxes are coloured with distemper as required." [1]

Cheney in *The Art Theatre* also describes a set of interchangeable units. " Such a setting," comments Ridge, " is cheaper than a good complete set of curtains, and far more useful for general work."

Besides the non-representational screen-flats used to build

---

[1] C. B. Purdom.

up abstract settings, screens in the more conventional sense of the term can often be employed. If stylized, they would make a suitable background for eighteenth-century plays. (See a screen setting for *The Marriage of Figaro*, Cheney, Plate CXXIV.) Plate XIII. shows a screen setting used for a school production of *The Mikado*. The wing-flats were painted in a very lovely green, stippled with gold; the back-screens were painted with ochre and Dutch " pink " and umber, toned down with some aniline dye, to produce a painted-silk effect.

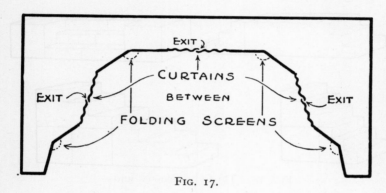

FIG. 17.

A Simple Screen Set.—Those who work on a very modest scale may manage with screens and very little else. Fig. 17 shows the plan of an all-purposes portable " set," consisting simply of folding screens (say 8 feet high) and curtains on rods. As a substitute for front curtains other screens can be slid across.

Three-dimensional Units.—The value of plastic units, particularly in conjunction with curtains and screens, has already been stressed, and is well illustrated by Plates I. and XII. The main thing to emphasize is that where these units are made for permanence they should be *units*; sets of steps should fit one another, and also the portal openings in the flats (see Fig. 16, C, D, E). Fig. 18 suggests simple re-arrangements of such units. They may well be covered with canvas. The unit idea, of course, can be carried too far. A firm flight of steps is better than one made up of various boxes (probably warped), balanced precariously on one another.

Windows and doors should be decently made ; a trim to suggest thickness greatly helps the illusion of solidity. Ply-wood is a better covering for the door than canvas. Doors

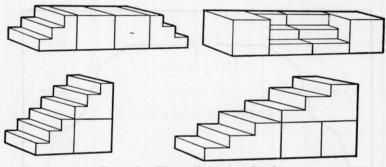

FIG. 18.—Three-dimensional units.

should normally be designed to open *outwards* from the set. Doors and fireplaces will need a backing-screen (of canvas or hessian) placed behind them, to prevent the audience seeing through into the wings.

" **Profile** " **Pieces.**—These serve a variety of uses—from the deliberately flat formalizations of trees, or house-ends (or it may be horses or ships—see the section on " Ballads," or even schoolboys—see the amusing instance on Plate VII.), to the more realistic ground-rows of mountains or distant landscapes set at the foot of the back-cloth. The Chauve-Souris, again, or the Arts League of Service, or Joan Lupton's Children's Theatre will provide rich examples. As for the ground-rows

[*Photo by Ladislaw.*

PLATE XII.—Prologue to *The Road to Emmaus* : *In the Cool of the Evening.*
Moira House School, Eastbourne.

[*Photos by Author.*]

PLATE XIII.—Examples of cheaply-constructed furniture made in the school craft-rooms from the (there may be several, each separately lit, if you have room, but this is unnecessary if you have studied the effects of light on colours), inspiration should be sought from the railway poster, not the Academy picture. Eschew details ; go for broad conventionalized effects.

All these silhouette pieces are made by attaching 3 mm. plywood to timber frames built to the most convenient shape (butt joint, corrugated fasteners, plywood keystone reinforcement). Ground-rows are supported by a hinged triangular prop.

Furniture.—Wherever possible, the furniture for the show should be made in the school craft-rooms ; a stock of useful pieces will soon be accumulated which a little ingenuity can accommodate to the purposes required. (Plates VIII., X., XI. may suggest how material can be used over again.) Some kind of " unit system " will be found an economy ; small tables should fit together to make a long one ; chairs of the same size may be arranged as a bench, etc., etc. It is surprising how cheaply articles can be constructed ; an armchair in the modern block-style, for instance (as in Plate IX.), can be built from 2-inch by 1-inch redwood (at $\frac{1}{2}$d. a foot) and plywood (at 1s. 6d. a 5-foot by 4-foot panel) for a total cost of less than 2s. And see Plates XIII. and XVI.

Specific Construction.—With the specific construction of the various scenic units I shall not deal. At long last a really useful book dealing with stage construction has appeared— *Stage Scenery and Lighting*, by Selden and Sellman (Harrap, 12s. 6d.). It is utterly practical down to the minutest detail, yet finely informed by the modern outlook—the work of an artist as well as a technician. It will save its cost several times a year.

Making a " Flat."—I shall, however, deal with the plain flat, because this is useful for so many purposes—as part of a set, as a leaf of a screen, as a wing piece for opera. (If you use wing flats—and they are useful when big entrances for chorus are needed—make them formal, not representational.) Its construction can be seen from the back view of those in Fig. 19. Three-inch strips of 1-inch timber form the basis. Corner joints can be mortise and tenon, or, simpler, butt or mitre joints held by corrugated fasteners. These are reinforced usually by corner-blocks or keystones of tough three-ply veneer or of metal.

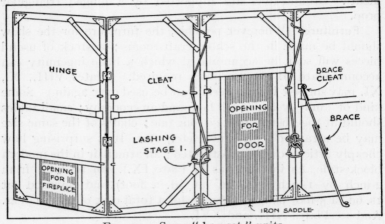

FIG. 19.—Some " box-set " units.

Canvassing.—Scene canvas for covering the frames costs about 2s. a yard (72 inches). Thinner materials—*e.g.* unbleached calico or balloon cloth—are cheaper, but not in the long run. (They slit when painted.) Coarser stuff—*e.g.* hessian—is useful for flats not in full gaze of the audience, such as backing-screens.

If it has not been treated before purchase, canvas may be fireproofed by spraying with a saturated solution of alum, or a 40 per cent. solution of sodium silicate, or the following : 1 lb. borax, 1 lb. sal-ammoniac, 3 quarts water.

To fix the canvas, tack it on to the face of the frame close
to the inside edge (as in Fig. 20)—but not to any cross-pieces—
starting from the middle and stretching, not too tightly,
towards the ends.   Having tacked the ends, turn the cloth back
over the tacks and glue the frame with hot glue (2 parts ground
glue, 6 parts water, plus 1 part whiting to prevent discolora-
tion).   Then press the canvas over the glue, swabbing it with
hot water till the glue works right through, when it will rub
up white.   When dry, the canvas should be trimmed off with a
sharp edge.   Some people drive the tacks in only half-way,
and remove them with pincers after gluing.

 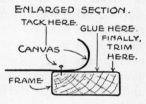

FIG. 20.

Assembling and Strutting.—Flats which have to be hastily
assembled or dismantled are lashed together (as in Fig. 19), the
rope running over cleats of wood or metal.   (Finish lashing off
with slipknot, to undo at a pull.)   Two-way hinges of the loose-
pin type can sometimes be used (Fig. 19).   For some connections carriage-bolts with wing-nuts are useful.   Large flats
(*e.g.* for arches) may be hinged for folding about their centre
line.

Flats needing support are usually strutted by an adjustable
metal brace which screws into the stage floor (Fig. 19).   Sometimes, with fixed sets, we strut ours from the top to the side
walls to allow more floor space in the wings.

Scene-painting.—To close the pores of the canvas for
painting, it must be primed with a coat of whiting and size

(*e.g.* 1 lb. whiting, 1 lb. glue size, 1 gallon water) applied warm with a large brush. This tightens up the surface considerably.[1]

When this is dry, painting can commence. Scene-paints are bought in powder form. (Write to Brodie and Middleton's, Long Acre, for tint schedule, price list—and any advice.) Mix one-third part glue size with two-thirds water, heat up in a bucket, and then stir in the paint, adding whiting (or black pigment) until the exact shade is reached. (*N.B.*—(*a*) It dries half as light again, so try it out on a piece of paper. (*b*) Too much whiting gives a chalky effect.) Its consistency should be about that of cream. If too sloppy it will not hide the canvas. If it has too much glue it will crack after drying ; if too little, it will powder off. If correctly mixed, the paint and size will set in a thin jelly overnight, and must be warmed up over a gas jet. (Use two pails—double boiler fashion—to avoid burning, and stir.) Mix enough to do the whole job, and stir frequently during use.

The modern scenic artist works in tones, and to secure richness he builds up each tone from its several colour elements. Instead of putting on a flat wash of, say, green, he will cover the canvas with little spots or blotches of blue, yellow, and perhaps different shades of green, " spattering " it on from his brush by flicks of the wrist. This is best done with the scenery flat on the ground. Such a surface will be susceptible to various effects under different lighting conditions. (Never paint till your lighting-plot is worked out !) The colour painted should be " conceived as an undertone of what it will seem when lighted on the stage." [2]

---

[1] Polunin (*The Process of Continental Scene-painting*. Beaumont. 1927) recommends a priming made from plain flour, water, and dissolved French glue, as being much kinder to bright or delicate colours, but very susceptible to chemical proofing. Polunin painted most of the big canvases for the Russian Ballet, and his book is concerned with that kind of work, but none the less it should be read ; his notes on the qualities of the various colours of scene-paint are most helpful.

[2] Simonson in *Encyclopædia Britannica*, 14th Edition.

This "broken colour" process is particularly appropriate for use with a system of screens.

Texture may be suggested also by "stippling"—dabbing on a second colour or a deeper shade, or perhaps a gold or bronze powder—with a sponge. Sometimes a wrung-out cloth is rolled over the surface. Or the brush itself may be manipulated to give various effects.

Scenic ground-rows of mountains, etc., profit from a spattering of pale violet to soften their outlines with atmosphere.

Note for the "Old Guard."—Those who misguidedly want to paint "pictures" on their canvas should outline in charcoal and exaggerate the details. It may interest them to know that it was a rule of thumb amongst the old perspective scene-painters that the horizontal line of sight should be fixed at 6 feet from the stage ; this gave an appearance of correct perspective from all parts of the hall.

Dyes.—Aniline dyes can also be used. The grains of aniline should be dissolved in warm water to the required strength, and a little Glaubers salt added as a mordant. The canvas (or costume material) should be dipped in and kept continuously moving. Dyes are brilliant only when used pure ; when mixed, they give muddy results. Canvas which is to be dyed should not be primed.

Dyes can be applied with brushes. They are not opaque, and therefore cannot be used to cover up old pattern, but they are useful to tone down painted scenery which is too garish.

Lenoir Rhyne College
LIBRARY

CHAPTER VI.—LIGHTING

" The function of light in the theatre is to stimulate the imagination."—SIMONSON.

" Light aids the actor in his interpretation of a character, it enhances the beauty of stage decoration, and as an art medium *per se* it carries to the spectator the mood, atmosphere, and emotional effect of the drama itself. . . . The non-professional lighting artist should be able to study a play and visualize an effect in light, not merely illumination in terms of batten-lights and spotlights, but something which grows out of the play itself and is a true expression of that play. He must think first in terms of æsthetic effect, and then he must be able to create it in terms of apparatus."—SELLMAN.

1. The Reform of Stage Lighting

In Chapter IV. we have noted the revolutionary character of modern stage decoration. In this revolution new developments of lighting have played a vital part.

Simplification ; Spiritual Intimation.—Lighting has helped the movement towards simplification. Light has become part of stage design, and, as Cheney remarks, " the beauty of light, even of richly coloured and varied light, is above all a simple beauty." And as the setting has become less and less realistic, so the spiritual and psychological qualities of light have been increasingly utilized. Emotionally, it has been said, we react to light more quickly than to any other medium in the theatre. " While a pillar and a candelabra, cunningly placed, might correctly suggest the whole cathedral in *Faust*, it was lighting that carried the deeper and spiritual intimation, the mood, the emotion of the place."

The Third Dimension.—Secondly, if the pictorial painted

background has become discredited in favour of the three-dimensional setting which shows the actor in the round as a living figure in space, it is largely because pioneers like Appia had shown the sculptural possibilities of light—of light controlled, light directed, light moulding form, suggesting depth, heightening shadow—all very different from the flat general illumination common on all stages thirty years ago, and still to be found on most. " We shall seek no longer," wrote Appia prophetically, " to afford the illusion of a forest, but only the illusion of a man in the atmosphere of a forest. . . . And when the trees, lightly stirred by the breeze, attract the attention of Siegfried, the spectators should see Siegfried bathed in light and living shadow, and not some stage ' cut-outs ' arbitrarily set in movement." See the utter simplicity of his designs for *Hamlet*—a few steps and a platform. Lighting creates the mood, the time, the place. Lighting changes the scenery.[1]

The Space Stage.—It is a small step from this to the modernist conception of the " space stage " where lighting replaces scenery almost entirely. Here the actor plays in a pool of light against a background of shadow—the action, as it were, focused into consciousness out of an infinity of time and space. Sometimes fragments of scenery may be included to give some kind of anchor to reality ; sometimes there is nothing but a dark surround of curtains. Or a scene vignetted in light in this fashion can be played on some clear area of a stage actually set for a realistic scene to follow.

Observe how the extremes of the space stage and full-blooded realism meet in *Cavalcade*. A spotlight picks out two or three figures ; isolates them in a world of shadows, excluding irrelevancies, denying distractions ; holds them, focused per-

[1] " The history of stage setting," says Simonson, " might almost be divided by B.A. as history in general is divided by B.C." Appia's own works (*La Mise en Scène du Drame Wagnérien* and *Die Musik und die Inscenierung*) are untranslated and virtually unobtainable. Appia was so far ahead of his time that the account of his beliefs in Simonson's book (*The Stage is Set.* 1933) forms the best chapter on modern lighting that has been written in English.

sonalities, clearly projected in the imaginations of the audience.
The scene over, the spotlight fades ; a momentary blackness ;
then the full stage lights swell up upon a crowded scene, and
individuality is temporarily submerged in the broader stream
of life.   There is no fall of curtain ; scarcely a pause.   There
is, however, more than a change of scene ; there is a change of
intimacy.   What the Elizabethan stage, with its apron projecting into the audience, could do to isolate personality, to
lend naturalness to soliloquies and self-communings, that we
can do, far more intensely, on our modern stages with light.

The Economy of Good Lighting.—I see no reason why
schools should not avail themselves of these advances in
technique.   As with scenery, so with lighting.   It costs very
little, if any, more to light your stage by units you can control,
than by the old-fashioned methods.   And—apart altogether
from its tremendous artistic possibilities—it is the great econ-
omizer ; it enables you, time after time, to " get away " with
almost anything in the way of scenery and costumes.   Mr.
John Hampden has described to the writer how his setting for
the witches' cavern in *Macbeth* consisted entirely of a few
dilapidated old rags of cheap material, fastened together almost anyhow with safety-pins, but made most impressive by
lighting.   Or mention may be made of a setting at the writer's
school for *The Discovery*, which was improvised in a few
moments at the lighting rehearsal, and was as effective as the
most costly scenery ; it consisted of some sections of the
gymnasium " box " (aided by a plank laid across to some
steps in the wings), which served for the poop, and a couple of
" flats " turned back to the audience to show the struts, and
laid horizontally—with a slight cant, to be exact—to represent
bulwarks.   A rail of sorts was knocked together from laths
and dowel rods.   The only item calling for careful design was
the poop lantern, and this was a mere frame of plywood and
orange-coloured tissue, containing a bulb.   The lantern was

PLATE XIV.—Setting for *Faust,* by Lee Simonson,
New York Theatre Guild.

The " spiritual intimation " of lighting.

[Photo by Author.

PLATE XV.—*R.U.R., Epilogue.* The Laboratory. Dawn.

(See pages 110, 111, and 114.)

the key to the lighting. A deep amber spot, fairly high in the wing, cast a shaft of light across stage, so that it picked out the faces of the players ; the illumination *appeared* to proceed from the lantern. None of it fell on the setting or on the black velvet surround. Some very dim blue footlights were used, and spotlights placed on the floor near the proscenium sent dim blue horizontal beams along the fore-stage, diffusing the whole scene with " atmosphere."

2. The Elements of a Lighting System

The keynote of lighting equipment should be flexibility. The *direction, colour,* and *intensity* of every ray of light cast upon the stage must be, in any ideal system, under absolute control. This is impossible where the illumination is afforded, as in the older theatre, mainly by rows of electric bulbs " penny plain, twopence coloured," throwing indiscriminate light in all directions.

1. The *direction* of the rays is determined (*a*) by their source —*i.e.* the position of the lamp ; (*b*) by the type of apparatus holding the lamp. We may distinguish (i) *batten-lights*—a row of lamps fixed in a batten, usually furnished with a reflector ; originally of the open or " trough " type, now usually made in smaller sections and divided off into compartments to take colour screens. (See the " old " and the " new " in Fig. 21.) Used for footlights, overhead lights, and (rarely nowadays) sidelights. (ii) *Floodlights*—a powerful lamp in a ventilated steel or tin box, with guides for colour-screen in front. (Really an isolated compartment of the modern batten-light on a large scale.) Both (i) and (ii) give a wide arc of illumination. (iii) *Acting-area floods* are floodlights hooded to restrict the spread of light to a given area. (iv) *Spotlights,* or focus lamps, concentrate the rays through a lens into a narrow beam.

2. *Colour* is determined by the colour of the lamp bulb or (far preferably) by a screen of glass medium or gelatine placed in front of it.

3. *Intensity* depends (*a*) on the type and power of bulb ; (*b*) on the reflecting power of the container ; (*c*) on the dimming which can be effected by a resistance in the circuit.

In an ideal system every lamp will have its own removable colour-screen, every circuit its own dimmer.

Let us briefly consider the main sources of illumination.

Footlights, or " floats," owe their traditional importance

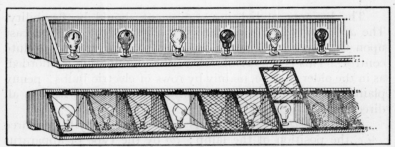

FIG. 21.—The " old " and the " new."

more to historic circumstance than to modern utility. If too strong they throw the actor's face into unnatural relief, and cast multiple shadows of the players upon the scenery and (far worse) the " sky." On small stages they are especially dangerous, as they are usually very close to where the actors play. For a full-lit scene you cannot dispense with them entirely—unless you are using front lights (see page 108)—because the main illumination from overhead will cause unnatural shadows under chin, nose, and eyebrows if left to itself. Strong side lighting may modify but will not obviate the trouble. Footlights, therefore, should be used as a correction, and as that only. They will usually need to be very dim.

Side Lights.—Upright battens are obsolete. Floodlights (on metal stands, or suspended) close to the proscenium give a cross-stage light that corrects some of the flatness of front lighting. Side floods in the wings bring out the third dimension. They give form. They can flood draperies with colour in a formal setting, or suggest sunlight pouring through a window in a realistic setting. Satisfactory side flooding requires adequate wing space. If the floods are too near the acting area the edges of the beam are defined upon the draperies or flats. (Care must be taken that actors waiting their turn do not interpose their persons.)

Spotlights are sometimes operated from the wings, but they need to be fairly high. Occasionally, to create a mist of light for some special purpose, we shine them horizontally along the stage floor itself ; this is, doubtless, quite unorthodox.

Overhead Lights.—The main type overhead used to be the batten-light, of which you might find anything from three to twenty rows. It is now invariably supplemented, if not supplanted, by floodlights, acting-area floodlights, and spotlights. The acting-area floods (which serve as baby-spots without lenses) are hung directly over the place they specially illuminate. The spotlights are gathered as near to the proscenium as possible, fixed to a rail or batten or a " light bridge," from which they can rake the whole stage. If you have enough of them you can scrap most of your other overhead stuff. If overhead lights are pulleyed to the roof they can be lowered between Acts for changes of colour screens (see Fig. 22). The usual fault is to use too much overhead light in an attempt to " kill " the unnatural shadows caused by overpowerful footlights. Balance is what is needed : the use of dimmers makes adjustment simple.

Back-lighting.—The back-cloth needs special lighting. The farther back it is the easier the problem, and the better the results. (If you had a cyclorama dome you would scrap your

borders and light it from lamps placed just behind the pelmet.)
On small stages it is necessary to arrange the lights as in Fig. 22,
so that the overheads and footlights cast no direct light on the
cloth. It is then lit by flood-battens overhead (as far from the
cloth as is practicable) and at the base. If there is no trough
in the stage floor for the base lights a "ground-row" of
scenery (a "terrace" is useful) serves to screen them. Big
floods (say 1,000 watt) can be used with advantage at either
side of the cloth as well. Mr. Harold Ridge recommends as

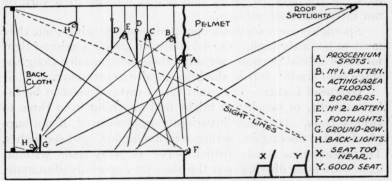

FIG. 22.—Lighting the stage.

much illumination being used on the back-cloth as upon the
whole of the main stage, if shadows are to be avoided.

In Fig. 22 I have drawn the sight lines of a spectator. Such
lines should be drawn accurately on scale drawings both for
lighting (elevation) and scenery (plan), and from all extreme
positions in the hall.

Front Lights are lights fixed beyond the proscenium attached
to vantage points in roof or gallery, and are much in favour
in the commercial theatres nowadays. The main objection is
to the shadows cast by the more horizontal beams. Long
throws necessitate lime or arc lamps. Schools can ignore

these, but a few simple spotlights fairly near the proscenium (as in Fig. 22) will be found most useful. Care should be taken that the light from them falls entirely *within* the proscenium frame. As such lamps will be inaccessible during the perform-ance, focus and colour must be fixed beforehand.

Strip-lights.—When a box-set is used it is unfortunate if the doors seem to lead into outer darkness, so that the faces of the characters are obscure at the moment of their entry or exit. It is therefore usual to use a small strip-light—a single compartment light, or a bulb or two on a small batten—which is hooked up (probably on the back of a flat) in a con-venient position just outside the door. The exact strength and position of the light—if unwanted shadows are to be avoided—must be found by experiment.

Spotlights must not be confused with the absurd limes that follow music-hall artists in their gyrations round the stage. As we have advocated them they are fixed, and, for the most part, unperceived by the audience. Their potentialities (as the next section may suggest) are almost unlimited.

3. Emphasis, Shadow, and Colour

"**General**" **Illumination and** "**Specific.**"—A distinction is sometimes made between " general " and " specific " illumina-tion. General illumination for the most part falls on actor and setting alike. It can suggest time and natural phenomena, but its effect is flat. " It can vary in intensity and colour, but has very little form." " If a stage 25 or 30 feet deep," says Simonson, " is flooded with an even radiance, nothing will persuade the eye that it is anything than a shallow box, how-ever suggestive the arrangement of the setting itself may be." [1]

Specific illumination is that cast upon a restricted area ;

[1] *Encyclopædia Britannica*, 14th Edition.

it throws shadows ; it creates relief ; it paints with colour ; it subordinates the unessential elements of the setting ; it concentrates attention to the centre of interest. Its chosen instrument is the spotlight. Used by itself the spotlight gives the conditions of the " space stage " ; used in conjunction with general illumination it gives subtle emphasis where it is needed —a touch of high light here, a table or chair picked out there ; sometimes it will be kept on throughout the scene, sometimes it will swell up just for a moment to record the expression on an actor's face at some critical point. You cannot have too many spotlights !

Light and Shade.—The question of shadow demands a further note. While accidental shadows are the producer's curse, deliberate shadows are his opportunity. " Without shadows," said Appia, " there can be no light." They can convey an impression of the physical solidity of the setting ; they can suggest the natural source of illumination ; [1] they can form a definite part of the decorative pattern of the scene ; and they can carry profound emotional significance. It is this emotional or symbolic use of shadow that is most fascinating ; a shadow slinking along a wall is, as Sellman says, more expressive of fear and danger than the figure itself. " And, if this shadow is increased in size by placing the light source below, the ominous and evil foreboding expression of the character is definitely magnified." The best example which the writer remembers occurred in the film *The Student of Prague*. Terence Gray's use of shadow in *Richard III*. has become a classic instance (Ridge. Fig. 69). The illustration of the setting for " the laboratory," in the fourth Act of *R.U.R.* (Plate XV.), shows how shadow can enable the minimum of stage property

[1] Though do not expect shadows, say, of a window frame, cast by a lamp a few yards outside, to look identical with those cast by the parallel rays of the sun. We found this difficulty so acute when our rising sun penetrated the big windows of our *R.U.R.* set (sending shadows *upwards* almost to the ceiling), that in place of a plain flat of our original design we substituted the black velvet panel to absorb *all* shadow (Plate XV. and Frontispiece).

to carry the maximum of suggestion. A small bench-light, low down, throws fantastic shadows of apparatus upon the wall. (Unfortunately this was not arranged as well for the photograph as it was for the show, but the general effect is conveyed.)

Colour.—Even more profound is the emotional significance of colour. Indeed, the whole problem of colour is so important that some discussion of its fundamentals is necessary.

The Theory of Coloured Light.—There is no such thing as pure white light. Daylight itself is a mixture of (literally) all the colours of the rainbow—*i.e.* of its spectrum. In artificial white light the colours are not mixed in the same proportions ; which accounts, of course, for the apparent change of colour of objects taken from daylight to artificial light—they are no longer reflecting the same wave-lengths. On the stage artificial white light, even from the newer gas-filled lamps, produces a hard glare which is both trying and unnatural. Even for artificially lit interior scenes " white light " will not do—pale amber or rose lamps or filters must be used to soften the effect. But no single colour can give the diffuse richness of daylight.

" White light " on the stage is therefore best produced by mixing together its constituents, the spectrum colours. In the famous Schwabe system all seven colours (or very close approximations to them) are employed, but for ordinary purposes it is sufficient to work with the three primaries—the three principal colours in the spectrum of daylight, which can themselves be combined to give white light—green, blue, and red. (The pigment artist regards the primaries as being yellow, blue, and red, but for him colour mixing is an absorptive or subtractive process—the primaries combine to give black ; mixing with light, on the other hand, is an additive process— the primaries combine to form white.)

The colour-wheel (Fig. 23) gives the key to the principles of mixing. Colours opposite (or " complementary ") to one another (*e.g.* blue-green and red) tend to neutralize each other, producing a grey effect. (Strictly, complementaries combine to produce a white light, though it has effects on coloured objects very different from daylight. Where a subdued atmosphere is appropriate, complementaries can be employed with effect from opposite sides of the stage, white high lights

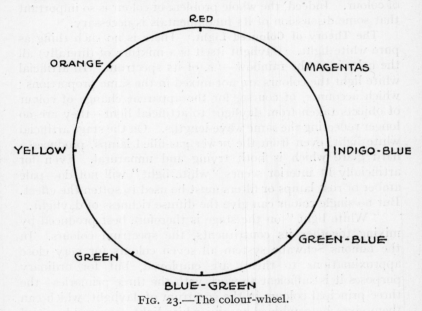

FIG. 23.—The colour-wheel.

and beautifully coloured shadows resulting.) A mixture of two primaries produces a secondary (*e.g.* red + blue = magenta ; green + blue = blue-green), and the secondaries in turn can combine to produce a primary (*e.g.* magenta + blue-green = blue).

Practical Application.—Now if your footlights, batten-lights, and so on, are built up of green, red, and blue lights,

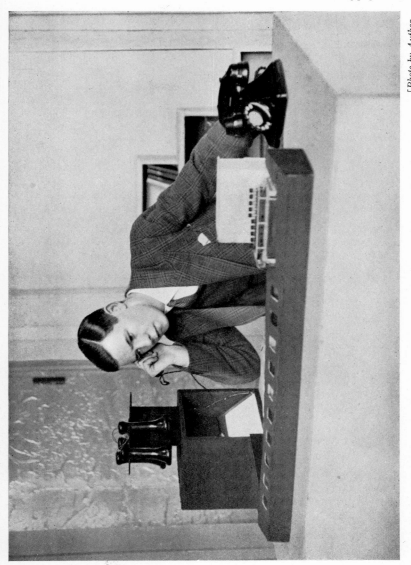

[Photo by Author.

PLATE XVI.—A simple desk, made exciting by the suggestion of television.

then it is possible, by strengthening one colour or dimming another, to produce almost any combination under the sun. (Ridge says that with seven colours, assuming ten dimmer positions to each colour, you can obtain 19,487,170 colour combinations ! He prints a valuable table showing dimmer settings to produce a large number of combinations with three colours.)

Such is the theory. In practice, because of the cost of obtaining the comparatively pure colour filters used by Ridge, it is more usual to work on four circuits—the additional colour being yellow. Our compartment battens, which are made in handy sections of ten lamps each, are all wired in two circuits, so that by using two battens side by side, whether overhead or for lighting the back-cloth (top or base), we can obtain a mixture of four colours. (On small stages " like " colours need to be fairly close together, that mixing may be effected near to the light source.) A fully equipped stage would have these batten sections independently wired, so that one colour could be mixed at one side of the stage, another in the middle, and a third the other side, but such refinements mean complicating the switchboard and running up costs.

Colour Filters.—In Little Theatres, where the battens are in position almost permanently, it is found most economical to equip the lamps with filters of coloured glass. For occasional purposes, however, gelatine is quite good enough, though it is apt to wrinkle, to crack, and to fade. (It can be obtained from The Strand Electric Company, 24 Floral Street, for $7\frac{1}{2}$d. a sheet, 22 inches by $17\frac{1}{2}$ inches. Write and ask for a specimen colour card. There are also more expensive brands.)

Gelatine is made in so many beautiful shades that it is possible to obtain most of the colours you need upon the stage without recourse to the mixing described above—for even if you have a number of dimmers you cannot always spare them for this purpose. But remember that you cannot go round changing filters in the footlights in the middle of a scene, or even between scenes, and usually you cannot do much changing with overhead lights either.

It is not always necessary that the filters employed in one circuit should all be the same. If you had only two circuits overhead you might have one consisting of green and blue, and perhaps some white; the other of rose, and straw, and amber. By varying the relative strength of two such circuits you could modify the general " warmth " of the illumination.[1]

The main lesson to learn from the three- (or four-) colour theory is never to use one colour only. If you have no dimmers at all you must experiment with gelatines of varying intensities. Pale amber, rose, and a little steel blue will give good general illumination.

Effect on Scenery.—When coloured light is used the effect of it on costumes, make-up, and painted scenery must be borne in mind. The usual principles of colour-mixing (subtractive, not additive as with pure light) apply. Rouged cheeks in a moonlight blue will appear indigo, a green dress in a red light almost black.[2] There is a well-known stage illusion which illustrates the point, where you see a warm room change before

---

[1] We once succeeded in mixing some dozens of hues with the use of four dimmers only. We were producing a dawn, seen through tall windows (Plate XV.). Overhead the back-cloth was lit with deep blue, which gradually changed to light blue. (That, of course, took two extra dimmers ; but we can ignore those.) At the base we wanted to suggest the dawn spreading across the heavens—we wanted to avoid a uniformly coloured sky. We had two batten sections, each in two circuits, arranged thus :

1. (a) deep blue	d. blue	d. blue	d. blue	d. blue.	
(b)	pale rose	amber	lemon	amber	p. rose.
2. (a) lemon	p. rose	lemon	rose	d. rose.	
(b)	rose	d. rose	d. rose	purple	purple.

1 (a) held the field at first, then 2 (b) suggested the flush spreading from the east ; 2 (a) carried on the good work, and finally 1 (b) established the day. Meanwhile, to complete the narrative, other dimmers were bringing up some overhead light on the stage itself, and controlling a spot which (carefully avoiding the back-cloth) presently caught the gauze of the windows with a mist of sunshine. Needless to say, it required more than one lighting rehearsal to synchronize this with the text. But to have produced the same effect by the mixing of independent hues would have been incomparably more complicated.

[2] See also page 142 for emphasis by colour.

your eyes to a ghostly forest. Both scenes are painted on the same canvas—the wood in red, the room in green. The red light flooding the room eliminates the red outline and shows the green one up in black; the green light in the forest scene produces the reverse effect. (Try this on a model stage—only see that your paints exactly match the colours of your lights.)

Many beautiful effects can be obtained with coloured light and shadow upon curtains or white scenery in abstract settings. The possibilities of the "broken-colour" method of scene-painting have already been described. The setting can be flooded with a different colour for each scene (the colour appropriate to the mood of the scene), while the actors are illuminated by lights confined to the acting area.

The Psychological Effect of Colour.—Colour, however, must never be used simply for its own sake. The play must always be the thing. Apart from the use of colour to suggest the light of nature—sunlight, moonlight, the chill cold light of dawn, the cosy warmth of evening, etc., etc.—its main value is psychological. Colour has a powerful subconscious effect on the mind. The subtle introduction of colour changes to suit the mood of a play enormously increases the chance of its "making contact"—a little extra rose flooded in during one scene to suggest health and spirits, a little more blue in another of a more melancholy cast, some greenish yellow in a scene of anger or jealousy, some generous purple to accompany the pomp of power in another. The audience will not (and should not) be consciously aware of these changes at all; it will impute their effect to the acting.

Colour Symbolism.—The more direct symbolic possibilities of colour should not be overlooked. In *R.U.R.*, to take what the reader must by now find a familiar example, we tried to associate the Robots definitely with a colour (fire-red) and a sound (the rhythm of machinery). Thus, in the first Act (Plate IX.), whenever the door leading to the factory was opened a red glow appeared upon its metallic (silver paper !) surface, and the rhythmic stamping of machines (from a radio-gramophone) was heard.   Then at the end of the third Act, when the Robots rose and overwhelmed the factory, the sky became flooded with fire-red, growing ever in intensity as the stage lights gradually faded until the Robots were in silhouette against it ; at the same time the sound of machinery rose to mingle in crescendo with wild music (" Pacific, 231 ") as the Robots marched to their labour and their leader was left alone against a livid sky.   For the encore curtain the stage was bare, except for the dead humans, the sky was still intense fire-red, and the music had given place to the steady rhythmic beating of the machines again at work.   The Robots were supreme.

4. Balance

The most important thing in lighting is to achieve correct balance—between the decorative or dramatic values, for instance, or between general illumination and specific.   (For example, if your spotlights cast harsh shadows on the faces, increase your general illumination.)   The wisest thing on the subject has been said by Norman Marshall : " It is easy enough to light a scene so that the actors' faces are clearly visible—an absolute essential except in the briefest scenes ; it is not difficult to light a scene for ' atmosphere ' and pictorial effectiveness ;   the real test of good stage lighting is the extent to which it succeeds in combining these two principles."

5. The Lighting Plot

The producer, having conceived the lighting " in terms of æsthetic effect," must proceed " to create it in terms of apparatus."   This involves the preparation of the " lighting plot " with which he furnishes the electricians. (If the lighting is complicated, and likely to make demands on the existing apparatus, or require the purchase or manufacture of additional equipment, it is advisable for him to prepare a general description of the effects he cherishes, and to discuss these " in terms of apparatus " with those who are looking after the electrical

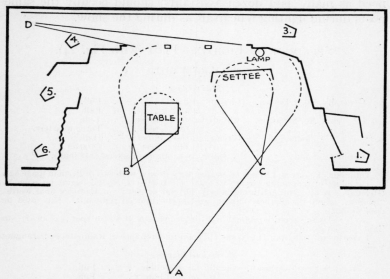

Fig. 24.—Diagram of " specific " lighting, showing spotlights, strip-lights, side-floods. (See Plate X.)

side ; he can evolve a detailed plot subsequently.) The original plot may be modified during the lighting rehearsals, but it must be ready in substance beforehand. A specimen section of an actual lighting plot (for the Act described on page 116) is appended.

From the plot can be prepared the cue-sheets for the individual electricians—operators of dimmers, and minders of flood lamps which require colour changes. For some shows (say, a revue, with perhaps twenty items each needing different lighting) these cue-sheets will be of great importance. They should be pasted on cards and hung on the lamp-stands, or wherever is most convenient. It is essential, of course, that the various " electricians " (and the master in charge may need as many as a dozen assistants) should occupy the same posts during lighting rehearsals as during the show.

Specimen of Lighting Plot (with Fig. 24).

" R.U.R," Act III.

Main Stage

General.	No. 1 Batten.	Circuit (a) rose	.	.	.	Full.
		(b) amber	.	.	.	Full.
	No. 2 Batten.	Circuit (a) rose, amber		.		Full.
		(b) blue, green	.		.	Three-quarters.
	Floats.	Circuit (a) rose, amber		.		Half.
		(b) blue, green	.		.	Quarter.
Specific.	Spots.	A (full) ; B, C (three-quarters) ; D (half).				

Dimming of No. 1 and Floats (a) begins, very slowly, with exit of Berman (page 82).

Dimming of remaining circuits (Floats (b), Batten 2, Spots) begins on page 85 (Helena's scream), and continues slowly till end of Act ; on Radius's final words, " Robots, march ! " all these circuits are slowly dimmed right out. This must be done *steadily*.

(*Note.*—There should be enough light from Spots A, B, C—or spot A alone (?)—to light Alquist during his final words.

Experiment with Spot D to come up again to catch face of Radius as he harangues mob.)

Back-cloth Lighting

No. 3 Batten (overhead).	Circuit (a) deep blue	.	.	Full.
	(b) mid blue	.	.	Full.

Circuit (b) dimmed on page 85 (with others above).

Circuit (a) dimmed right out (slowly, steadily) on Radius's final words, so that the only light is that from the base red.

No. 4 Batten (foot). Circuits (a) and (b). Blues used in Act II. removed during interval two, and replaced with fire-red. . . Out.

No. 5 Batten (foot), one circuit. Fire-red. . . . . Out.

Bring in 4 (a) slightly, after lamp goes out (page 85), and then welling up behind smoke which follows explosion. This need not be uniform ; use liquid dimmer.

Bring in 4 (b) after second explosion (page 86, foot).

Bring in 5 on page 88, when Radius begins to harangue mob. Gradually increasing to full intensity to curtain.

Side-floods (Nos. 3, 4). Blue . . . . Full.

Dim out during page 85. Insert fire-red slides. Bring up with Batten 5.

Strips

No. 1, rose.   No. 5, pale amber.   No. 6, rose.   All to be switched out after Berman's exit, page 82.

Table Lamp

Lights on page 64, when Fabry switches it *on* and *off* again.

Lights on page 85, when Fabry switches it on.   Must be turned off from switchboard *eight seconds after cue*, " A torch to be given from hand to hand, from age to age, for ever ! "

Note.—The actual colour numbers of the gelatines specified have been omitted from this plot because different makers employ different numbers ; they are essential to enable the electrician to order up supplies.   If the producer has no experience of the various colour values of gelatines (either on the stage or his model stage) he should experiment well in advance before ordering in bulk.

6. *Lighting Equipment*

For the school producer and his colleagues the phrase " creating in terms of apparatus " may take on a grimly literal meaning.   The art of grappling patiently with sheet-tin is not given to all.   Nevertheless much of the equipment may be made fairly simply, and at a mere fraction of its purchase cost.

Batten-lights.—If you are starting off from scratch, your problem is more straightforward than if you inherit, or have yourself already made (as we did in our early ignorance of the game), equipment of an obsolete nature.   We began by sticking rows of bulbs in open battens ; these illuminated the stage, the scenery, the borders, and the roof with complete impartiality.   Fig. 28 A shows the cheapest method of conversion to the compartment type, for use either overhead (as in the side elevation) or as footlights.   But a compartment per lamp is better—especially if your batten is wired in two circuits.   The type illustrated in A allowed four pieces of gelatine to be obtained from a sheet of the 22-inch by 24-inch size.

Fig. 25 illustrates an improved type.   We have made a number of these in sections of ten compartments each ; they

can be used at the base of the back-cloth, as footlights (though
Fig. 27 A shows a better position for lamps there), or overhead ;
upon occasion they can be used singly, but more often two or
even three sections are used end to end, bolted into one long
batten.

The base containing the lamp-holders is ½-inch timber ;
the sides are five-ply wood ; the compartment panels again are
½-inch wood. (These should be made from a template to

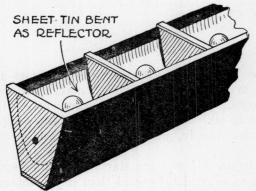

SHEET TIN BENT
AS REFLECTOR

FIG. 25.—A home-made compartment flood-batten.

ensure uniformity.) Pieces of strip wood tacked on make the
grooves which take the gelatine holders. Unless you are
extraordinarily good with tin, these holders are best made
professionally. (They will cost about 1s. each ; get a model
frame from some local theatre, and take it to a tinsmith for a
quotation.) Ours were designed to hold a quarter of a gelatine
sheet of the 22-inch by 17½-inch size. The reflector in these
compartments is a rectangular piece of tinned plate with a hole
cut in the middle of it, through which the lamp-holder passes ;
it is secured by a screw-ring such as holds a lampshade.

Fig. 26 shows a cheap way of making footlights. End-pieces and compartment pieces of $\frac{1}{2}$-inch wood are set up, as illustrated, upon a batten, and tinned plate is nailed over the framework. (A sheet of tin costing 5d. will cover three compartments. As for cutting it, if the school possesses no metal-working tools, use a pair of old grass shears, fixing the lower blade in a vice.) With a slight alteration in design, overhead batten-lights could be constructed in this way.

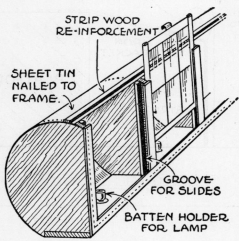

STRIP WOOD RE·INFORCEMENT

SHEET TIN NAILED TO FRAME.

GROOVE FOR SLIDES

BATTEN HOLDER FOR LAMP

FIG. 26.—Home-made footlights.

Fixing the footlights may cause some trouble; they should not stick up above the level of the stage floor. One method is to bracket them to the front edge of the stage. After various experiments we have built a trough, supported at the ends and centre by wrought-iron brackets screwed to the stage and supported by struts to the floor. Its distance from the stage can be made extendable, and canvas is used to fill in the gap. In it can be placed such footlight units as are required—sections of compartment battens, or isolated flood-boxes. Such a trough does *not* need to be as wide as the proscenium opening (see Figs. 27 A and 27 B).

Floodlights.—Fig. 28 B shows a flood-box to take a 100- or 150-watt lamp. It is made of thin tinned plate, japanned outside. We have had a large number specially made for us

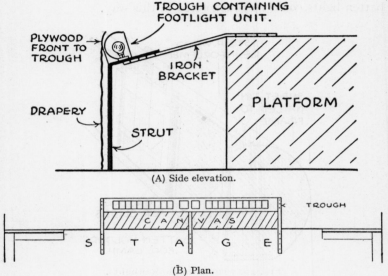

(A) Side elevation.

(B) Plan.

FIG. 27.—The footlight problem.

at a cost of only a few shillings each. We use them for lighting the back-cloth, as strip-lights or (with weaker lamps) as occasional footlight units. A curved reflector of steel, aluminium, or frosted glass can be added.

Fig. 28 C shows a 500-watt flood-box home-made from a biscuit tin. The reflector is tinned plate. The ventilation cut-outs are bent inwards, and outer coverings riveted on to prevent escape of light. These boxes must not be hung too

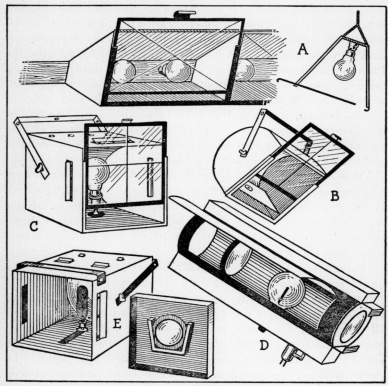

FIG. 28.—Types of lighting apparatus.

near curtains as they get very hot, and the lamp must not be too near the gelatine. For the outsides use a heat-proof enamel (*e.g.* Castle Brand dull " Blacquette "), or have them properly stoved. Notice the butterfly nut which holds the box at the required angle.

Spotlights.—Fig. 28 D shows a professional spotlight, and Fig. 28 E a home-made model, built in a biscuit box, with the lens (a simple plano-convex—half of a condenser unit) slotted into the lid (back view of which is shown). Focusing can be effected by moving the lamp (projection type) forwards or backwards in a groove. A parabolic mirror, borrowed from the Physics Laboratory, helps to concentrate the light. This is a luxury. (Such a mirror can, of course, be used to throw a beam without the help of a lens at all, but it will project an image of the filament upon the setting, so a projection lamp, which has its filament concentrated, should be used. The worst of projection lamps is that they are made to burn in one position only, and the horizontal type cannot be used vertically, and vice versa.)

Most spotlights give a beam of light which is surrounded by a fainter secondary beam (owing to the size of the light source). If this is a nuisance, it can be mitigated by affixing a tubular hood in front of the lens, though when we need a very defined beam we use a projector with condenser and focusing lens— sometimes the school lantern.

Dimmers.—Fig. 29 illustrates a home-made dimmer of the liquid type. These are not only far cheaper than the metal coil-resistance type, but are more satisfactory, especially for large voltages. It is useful to have a number of metal ones, all the same ; they are easier to handle, and can be " set " more accurately. Liquid dimmers can be made in large gas jars or in drain pipes sealed at one end. The liquid (the electrolyte) acts as a resistance to the current passing between two plates (the electrodes). As the plates are separated, the resistance is increased. The plates, of iron, should be of such a size that the current density does not exceed 1 amp. per square inch (*e.g.* 10 amp. current—10 square inch area of contact). This determines the minimum diameter of the containing vessel. The amount of liquid must be adequate to absorb the heat generated, or boiling will occasion unpremeditated thunder-storm effects on stage. (At least 1 cubic inch per watt for dimmers up to 10 amps. ; $\frac{1}{2}$ cubic inch per watt above 10 amps.)

This determines the height of the vessel. In practice, a gas jar 2 feet high and 6 inches in diameter will serve to dim any circuit up to 1,000 watts.

For electrolyte a solution of salt or soda may be used. (Sulphuric acid electrolyte, with *lead* plates, is *not* recommended; it is dangerous.) The salt or soda solution should be of such strength that the electrodes have to be separated to their fullest extent to bring the lights from full on to off. (Fill the jar almost full of water, suspend the top plate a few inches below the surface, switch on, and add salt or soda very slowly, allowing time to dissolve, until the lamps in the circuit just begin to glow. The salt or soda can be added in solution if the jar is not filled too high with water. Do not, by the way, add liquid to a live dimmer from a bucket or metal container without expecting to receive a shock.)

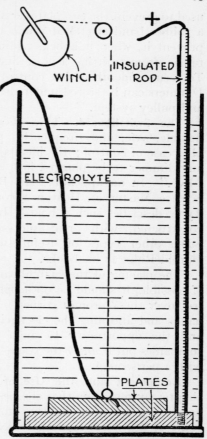

FIG. 29.—Home-made dimmer.

The bottom plate must be sufficiently heavy not to be lifted by attraction by the top one. Rubber washers can be used to prevent the two plates actually touching. (Incidentally, a rubber band stretched round the rim of the top plate will prevent it, when it knocks against the side of the glass container, from emitting a noise like an approaching fire-engine.) To secure smooth action control the separating by a handle. Dimmers can be stored under the stage and worked by a cable and pulley system.

The Switchboard.—The school switchboard needs to be flexible, safe, and (frequently) portable. " Flexibility " implies ease of control ; the ideal arrangement is one that allows any dimmer to be plugged into any circuit while the board is " live." In an appendix, Mr. H. Bambrough, M.Sc., Senior Science Master at Heaton Secondary School, Newcastle-on-Tyne, describes such a board—based upon one which he has constructed, with great success, for school performances. Some other types of useful switchboard are described by Harold Ridge in his books.

The placing of the switchboard may cause some difficulty. If possible, it should be on a lighting platform some 10 or 12 feet over the " prompt corner "—out of the way of the stage hands and affording the electrician a view of the acting area, and the opportunity to angle spotlights on to it. Some companies put it *under* the stage, and equip the poor electrician with a periscope.[1]

Equipment and the Use of It.—Let me conclude this chapter by repeating that the best apparatus in the world will not give good stage lighting unless it is properly employed. Some of the worst lighting I have ever seen on any stage—as well as some of the best—has been at the new Memorial Playhouse at Stratford !

---

[1] Jeffreys and Stopford make the interesting suggestion that it can be built into a cupboard on the side wall ; the cupboard may be locked when the equipment is not in use.

CHAPTER VII.—THE PERFORMANCE

1. The Stage Manager

THE professional producer concludes his duties after the dress rehearsal, when he hands over the reins to the stage manager. The school producer seldom escapes so lightly.

If a separate person is appointed to take over the full duties of stage manager he must make himself thoroughly familiar with the producer's work. He should have attended all the later rehearsals ; he must know the plot, the exits and entrances arranged, the changes of scenery involved, the disposition of stage properties, and such changes of lighting as involve physical alterations—movements of lamps or filters— on the stage itself. And he must not only know the mechanics of the business, he must try to understand the producer's underlying purposes.

In practice it is seldom worth while for another person to take all this trouble for the sake of one or two performances, and the producer, if he is not actually nominated on the programme as stage manager, will be at hand to supervise generally and to put those all-important finishing touches—the exact placing of cushions or flowers,[1] for example—which contribute so largely to the tasteful effect of scenes. The producer, however, should not actually take on the job of stage manager if it can be helped, as other duties, such as the supervision of

---

[1] Artificial flowers, it should be said, are very useful in neo-realistic settings ; they can " suggest " such a lot about the character of a room and its occupier, apart from providing a touch of colour to enliven a set. If they are set in a place (*e.g.* near a window) where sunlight may be presumed to fall, the illusion is much heightened if they are lit specially by a " baby-spot."

" make-up " and the final adjustment of costumes, and a score of emergency problems, will claim his attention during the evening.

The stage manager will learn the arrangement of scenery and the positions of stage furniture from the detailed drawings which will have been prepared. It is a happy arrangement if you can secure the colleague who has had charge of the making of the scenery to act as stage manager and supervise its erection on the stage. He will organize the storing of scenic units behind stage so that they are available with a minimum of dislocation when required. Flats, for example, should be marked clearly with Act and Scene on the back, and numbered to ensure their being set correctly (*e.g.* figure 2 on left of one flat joins figure 2 on right of another).

Several rehearsals may be necessary before the stage crew can do the job with sufficient slickness. Quietness, too, is as important as speed, especially when there is no orchestra for the intervals ; noise from the stage between scenes (*a*) sounds amateurish, (*b*) may wreck the emotional continuity of the play. Tennis shoes should be worn. Every member of the stage crew should be allotted a specific job for each change, whether dismantling or erecting scenery, or bringing on or off the portable units. Each chair, for instance, should be made a definite responsibility of one or other of the crew, who must also know at what stage of the proceedings he can move it without getting in the way of older people busy with other jobs.

The producer will supply the stage manager with a " property plot "—a list of all the movable " props " required for each scene, from settees to sandwiches. The stage manager will see that they all go " on "—and that they are fit to go on.

Hand properties necessary to the action, such as daggers, fans, revolvers, documents, purses, should be made the responsibility of the players who use them. If they are left on stage the players should collect them after the show in readiness for the next night. If a property, say a revolver, has to be used in different scenes by different people, definite arrangements must be made for the transfer or there will be last-minute panics. Letters or telegrams which are carried on should be labelled with the Act and Scene on the envelope, and some one must be made responsible for their return or replacement for subsequent performances.

Not the least of the stage manager's duties is to see that chemical fire extinguishers and buckets of sand are ready at various points.

2. *The Prompter*

It is best if the prompter attends rehearsals from the very beginning. He can act as a kind of secretary to the producer, making notes of instructions he delivers, and as a kind of " continuity girl." He may draft the " property plot," and should be in charge of props used during rehearsals. It should be his job to notify the producer each morning of people called for the day's rehearsals who are absent from school.

Serious use of him should be made during the performance. Verbal prompting—though he must always be on the *qui vive* for it—will probably form a small part of his activities. (Our prompter tells me that in the last two years he has given only eight prompts during some thirty hours' playing.) Incidentally, when prompting, he should stress not necessarily the *next* word, but some important word or phrase just ahead that is likely to restore the lost *idea* ; a prompt like " and then he——" is useless. But he prompts others besides the actors ; he is the nerve centre of the whole stage organization. Our prompter is fitted with a swivel reading stand to take the text (and/or score) so that his hands are free to operate a tiny switchboard which hangs at his side. One switch connects to a lamp at the back of the hall to signal " hall lights off " or " hall lights on " ; another gives the signal for curtain (" on " for several moments for warning ; " off " for action) ; another connects with the desk of the conductor out in front ; another is used for signals for " effects," etc., behind the scenes ; a final switch operates a bell in the " make-up " room to warn players to take up their positions in the wings—a code of rings distinguishing various groups of principals and chorus. The prompter marks all these cues in his prompt copy. This is infinitely more satisfactory, we find, than using a call-boy, who always gets mislaid. (All the same, a call-boy should be nominated ; an emergency messenger is often useful.)

The prompter should act as timekeeper, recording the time taken to play each Act each evening, and keeping the stage manager posted as to the progress of the interval. He should, of course, secure the stage manager's approval before actually signalling for the " warning " bell.

3. Effects

The importance of " effects " varies with the play, but they should always be carefully rehearsed, both for timing and intensity. The " effects man " (or " manager "—if you do The Ghost Train you will need a crew of a dozen !) should be supplied with a " plot," and can be warned by signal from the prompter when his " turn " is approaching.

The conventional methods of producing " noises off " are too well known to be described in full—a tin sheet shaken for thunder, a slatted wooden cylinder rotated under a tight length of canvas for wind, peas rolled in a tin box for rain, halves of a coco-nut clapped for hoof-beats, broken glass poured into a dustbin for a crash, etc., etc. Nowadays, how-

ever, advantage can be taken of the effects records made by
Columbia and H.M.V. They are seldom satisfactory with an
ordinary gramophone owing to the absence of volume control ;
a radio-gramophone should be used, or some special apparatus
made (preferably with two turntables and a mixing unit).
For unusual sounds ingenuity and experiment will usually
suggest a method. We were quite stumped once by the necessity to produce the sound of " very rapid typing " on the stage,
until some one hit on the idea of fixing an electric buzzer
inside the desk. It served perfectly.

Reference to the symbolic use of sound—sound as a kind of
leitmotiv—has already been made (Chapter VI., page 116).
There is an apt passage (quoted by Simonson) in a letter which
Eugene O'Neill sent to the producer of his play *Dynamo* : " I
cannot stress too emphatically the importance of starting early
in rehearsals to get these effects exactly right. It must be
realized that these are not incidental noises, but significant
dramatic overtones that are an integral part of that composition in the theatre which is the whole play."

4. Back-stage Organization ; " Make-up "

During the performance there should be strict discipline
behind the scenes. Talking to the prompter should be sche-
duled a criminal offence. The cast should not be allowed to
watch the play from the wings (it is unfair to the players on
the stage), and should not be tolerated in the wings longer than
is necessary. (With chorus in opera it is a good plan to signal
them up, if it can be arranged, while applause or a loud passage
will drown any noise. Put them in the right order before they
leave the waiting-room.) Our waiting-room is separated from
the stage door by a corridor. To ensure quiet we make it a
rule that waiting-room door and stage door shall never be open

both together, and there is an attendant on each door all the evening. This may sound finicking, but neglect of such details of organization may ruin the most beautiful or dramatic moments of the performance.

Arrangements off-stage will depend so much on the individual character of the building that no general recommendations can be made. It may, however, be helpful if I outline the organization adopted by my own school when a work involving a large cast is being performed.

On arrival—say ninety minutes before the show begins—the players go to a wardrobe room to draw their dresses, wigs, hand " props." These they return after each show. (This—storing, issuing, checking—is made one master's responsibility.) They then change (usually in the Physics Laboratories, because the flat-topped benches are useful for laying out dresses), and then they go for any final adjustment (hooks, eyes, ribbons, etc.) to a bevy of ladies who attend for the purpose in the Art Room (where the light is good). (If costumes are hired these adjustments may take considerable time on the first occasion, and special allowance should be made in fixing the times for dress rehearsal.)

When dressed, our players proceed to the dining-hall, which serves as " make-up " room and waiting-room. Four tables, each with special light (for " make-up " light should approximate as closely as possible to stage light), are each equipped with a box of " make-up " materials (renewed between performances) under the charge of expert enthusiasts, two or three per table. Players secure cold cream and ground colour from another table, and then report for the remaining stages to the experts as they have been previously instructed (e.g. certain principals, Table 1 ; other principals, Table 2 ; chorus 1–16, Table 3 ; chorus 17–32, Table 4). On the tables will be any illustrations available of the characters to be achieved, and perhaps a schedule prepared by the producer of numbers of grease-sticks and liners suggested for use, so that there may be some uniformity of hue and nationality in the chorus.

On the wall of this room hangs a large chart dividing the play into sections, numbered—a new entrance commencing a new section. An indicator (another individual's responsibility) shows the number of the section being performed upon the stage at any moment. To fortify any panic-stricken memories a diagram at the top of the chart shows all the stage entrances numbered, and the chart indicates the number of the entrance through which each character has to enter.

Such arrangements ensure the maximum of speed and the minimum of confusion ; they keep ladies out of the dressing-room, and keep the " make-up " room relatively free from the litter of cast-off clothes. (Quick changes can, of course, be made in it.) After the show, the players return their costumes *before* they smear themselves with removing cream.

This does not mean that boys should never be allowed to do their own " make-up." I believe most profoundly that they should have ample opportunity to practise at regular classes and at their leisure, and this should be a definite part of dramatic society work. Particularly should they attempt character " make-ups." For this they will find themselves forced to study in the flesh the type of character they are trying to create with paint. They may embarrass people in tramcars by staring too closely at their crowsfeet or the angles of their wrinkles, but they will be studying human nature. The " make-up " class may be as much a training in the humanities as work in the art room or the reading of Dickens. But when it comes to a show, such as an opera, with a large cast, speed and the problem of supplying material necessitate arrangements of the kind described.

The art of " make-up " is too technical for full discussion here. The books by Ward, Parsons, and Redglove and Fox should be consulted ; and the chapter in Jeffreys and Stopford is excellent.[1] The best way of learning the art is to watch experienced players performing on themselves, and to come away and attempt to do likewise. A few general suggestions may be offered :

Thoroughly wipe off the preliminary coat of cold cream (or, better, dispense with it entirely).

Accentuate vertical lines to secure long features ; horizontal lines and masses to secure broad features.

Place cheek patches high to suggest youth ; low to suggest sunken age.

Utilize natural wrinkles and contours as far as possible.

Accompany all shadows with corresponding high lights.

Use an orange stick for lining.

Study a Leichner price list for materials (numbers $1\frac{1}{2}$, $2\frac{1}{2}$, 5, 9, with carmines 1, 2, 3, and brown, lake, blue, and black liners will be found the most useful).

Wipe the " make-up " off with a towel *before* washing.

Remember that " make-up " in straight parts is simply to counteract the flat effect of lighting, so that modern lighting necessitates very little.

Observe the effect of the " make-up " at dress rehearsal from various positions in the hall.

5. *The Dress Rehearsal—and Other Matters*

The dress rehearsal should be as much like an actual performance as possible. The ridiculous superstition that " a bad dress rehearsal means a good show " belongs to an age when the theatre was not taken seriously. The ideal should be to avoid all interruption. Essential comment can be made at the end—and in general it will be found wiser at this stage

---

[1] The articles on the subject in *Theatre and Stage* look like superseding all these authorities.

to praise than to condemn. Of course, where the company finds itself acting for the first time in a strange hall, or, to a lesser extent, where it finds itself wearing strange costumes that need careful draping, or (in opera) singing to the accompaniment of a strange orchestra, then some interruption will be unavoidable.

" Curtains."—The taking of " curtains," if it is permitted, must be rehearsed. The professional habit of allowing the actors to acknowledge applause at the end of each Act cannot be too strongly condemned ; it ruins the emotional continuity of the play. " Act curtains," therefore, should be simply tableaux, " freezing " some dynamic grouping of the players. (Only occasionally will such curtains be appropriate ; a forced " poseyness " must be avoided.) " Final curtains " should muster the entire cast on stage ; the players should receive applause as a team, not as individuals.

Photographs.—If press photographers are invited to the dress rehearsal they should be given a time twenty minutes or so before it is due to begin ; they should not be allowed to interrupt the proceedings. Fortunately the use of flash-powder in press photography is obsolescent !

As for formal photographs for purposes of record, either a special occasion should be arranged, or they should be taken after one (or more) of the performances. To save time (and patience) the producer should decide beforehand exactly what is to be taken, have all groups (mentally) prearranged, and notify the cast—by means of a kind of call-sheet—of the " order of events."

The average professional photographer will make a sad mess of scenes upon the actual stage ; [1] he distrusts the use of stage light, and flash lighting from the front destroys the third dimension. Such photographs can only be taken adequately by

---

[1] Moira House did wisely to choose a genuine art photographer (Plates I. and XII.).

those who know the production intimately, while to produce the *effect* of the performance, the lighting, especially the colour, may have to be modified very considerably, even if panchromatic plates and colour filters are employed. Here is a job for the school photographic society ! Within a few years the necessary technical experience of colour values and exposures will be acquired.

The " School " Performance.—At some schools it is the custom to give a special performance, to which the pupils and their juvenile friends are admitted at specially cheap rates. Generally, such a performance should be held *before* the public performances, to give the players additional experience. But unfortunately—unless an attitude of reverence towards drama has been bred in the school—an audience of this kind is very difficult to play to if the work is at all profound, and may put the actors clean off their stroke. For some forms of entertainment a school audience is ideal ; for poetic drama, or the drama of ideas, it is better that pupils should experience the play in the more receptive atmosphere of a public performance. (An audience of *seniors*, of course, is another proposition.)

CHAPTER VIII.—COSTUME

" The costume has as important a function on the stage as the actor's face. . . . The costume, by its line, shape, and colours, is either an aid to an actor's movements or paralyses them. Costume either accentuates the transmission of the actor's emotions to the audience, or neutralizes or even destroys them. The costume suggests to the audience the ideas which guided the actor in his interpretation of the part. Even the best actor, in a costume which does not fulfil these requirements, is like a statue by a good sculptor on which some passer-by has put his overcoat, leaving the head alone uncovered."

KOMISARJEVSKY.

The Dramatic Society Wardrobe.—Every school should aim at acquiring a stock of stage costumes—Elizabethan, classical, miscellaneous—into which boys can delve to dress their own impromptu efforts. It is amazing to what different purposes the same costumes can be put. Some costumes which we made several years ago—simple, boldly-cut garments of serge, casement cloth, sponge cloth, etc.—for Bottom and his fellow-mechanics, have served us since for Greeks and Trojans in *X=O*, for some of Columbus' crew in *The Discovery*, for burlesques of classical dances, and for endless parts in ballads. Upon the same neutral basis, as it were, endless variations can be imposed—perhaps simply by a belt, or a cloak caught from the shoulder, or a pattern in *appliqué*—and lighting does the rest.

Costume as an Element in the Production.—But a stock wardrobe, for all its uses, will not carry a dramatic society very far, and it may become a positive nuisance by tempting the producer to dress his characters with the clothes he happens to possess, instead of the clothes that he conceives the play to demand. Ideally, every costume in a production should be designed specially for that production. Note that we say " production," not just " play." The costume must help to interpret the idea the producer has of the play—his fundamental conception. One producer's designs for a play would be useless to another producer. Realistic costumes would be fatal in a work interpreted as a fantasy ; bright colours out of place for characters conceived as morbid or melancholy. And hence the difficulty of acquiring costumes for a play " ready made." " It is infinitely preferable," says Komisarjevsky, " to act a play in some more or less commonplace dress which the audience can accept as a conventionality to be disregarded, than in the most magnificent pictorial, statuesque, or expressionistic costumes which have been devised by an artist independent of the idea of the production, and which neither express the meaning of the play nor correspond to the emotions and movements of the actors. . . . It is a well-known fact that certain plastic forms and certain combinations of colours produce definite effects on the human mind. Therefore the shape of costumes and the colour scheme of the ensemble of costumes should depend not solely on the characteristics of the *dramatis personæ*, or on decorative, pictorial, or sculpturesque ideas, but principally on those expressionistic effects and impressions which the producer wishes to create by the action of the play as a whole, and of each separate moment of that action."

We can distinguish, then, between the symbolic and the decorative uses of costume. Costume is both part of the actor—a visible extension of the personality he represents— and part of the setting. All that we have said (Chapter VI. 3) of the psychological suggestiveness of colour applies to costume ; at the same time costume must be envisaged together with grouping and scene—its line and colour must be woven into the visual pattern of the play. It must be appropriate to the

character, help to distinguish him from the other characters
and from the background (the movements of an actor in black
against a black curtain would be lost), and yet—unless it be
wished to suggest emotional discord—must harmonize and blend
with the whole environment.[1]

Hiring Costumes.—If, then, you are hiring costumes from
a theatrical costumier it is better to send along detailed speci-
fications (accompanied perhaps with colour drawings) than to
send along a general order for costumes for such and such a
play. A list of recommended costumiers is appended. They
will lend costumes—often truly magnificent—at an average
rate of about half a guinea a week. Usually they take good
care to see that the costumes sent blend well with one another—
but that is no guarantee that they will blend with your scenery.
Sometimes—*e.g.* for a Gilbert and Sullivan opera—there is no
option but to take the whole set " as provided." (Incidentally,

---

[1] The most stimulating example of symbolic costuming known to the writer is
contained in Stanislavsky's account of the Craig production of *Hamlet* at Moscow—
with the contrast between the Prince and the " golden Court." Milton Smith provides
an interesting coloured costume plate for *The Tempest.* He points out that the warm
colours—red, orange, and yellow—are appropriate for vigorous, passionate characters;
the cool colours—blue, green, and violet—suggest calmness and quietness; that
neighbouring colours (see the colour-wheel, page 112) suggest harmony and friend-
ship; while complementary colours indicate conflict and struggle. In *The Tempest*
he distinguishes three groups of characters: (1) Prospero, Miranda, and Ferdinand;
(2) King Alonso and the shipwrecked courtiers; (3) the comic characters, Stephano,
Trinculo, and Caliban. " For the first group cool colours are obviously appropriate,
representing the innocence and idyllic calmness of the love story. Prospero, however,
must be made severe and dignified; he was dressed in black trimmed with gold-
yellow. Miranda's dress was a quiet yellow, and Ferdinand wore a royal blue. So
that the costumes should harmonize, both were tipped a little towards green—that is,
Miranda's yellow was a slightly green-yellow, and Ferdinand's blue a green-blue.
The basic colour of the Alonso group was a red-purple—representing both the evil
passion of the group, and the royalty of the court group. All the courtiers were
dressed in varying shades of red and purple. The most prominent ones wore brightest
colours, which were ' cooled ' by the addition of green for old Gonzalo. There was
no element of monotony about these costumes, for each colour contains in itself an
infinite variety. Orange was chosen as the basic colour for the comic group: Stephano
wore a bright orange costume; Trinculo an orange, red, and yellow, made like the
conventional fool's costume; and Caliban, an orange-brown. Ariel, as a character
quite detached from any of the groups, wore varying costumes of different colours,
dependent upon the disguise he was for the moment assuming."—*The Book of Play
Production.* In their *Book of Dramatic Costumes* Edith Dabrey and C. M. Wise give
lists of the symbolic properties of colours, and diagrams to show blending. The
vagueness of colour nomenclature weakens the value of such aids.

through Messrs. Fox, you can get the actual costumes used by D'Oyly Carte before they adopted the new Charles Ricketts costumes ; one day, perhaps, these superb costumes will be available too.)

" To hire or not to hire " is often a difficult question. Costumes, like settings, may be the more convincing for being simplified, but they are so much part of the person of the actor that a certain degree of sartorial efficiency is essential. Our experience suggests that it is best to hire :

(*a*) All eighteenth-century costumes—which cannot possibly be made adequately by amateurs.

(*b*) All costumes which are not likely to come in useful for another show.

(*c*) All wigs. (Wigs cannot be home-made,[1] and good ones are very expensive to buy. A few cheap ones are useful for the stock box.)

Odd items of clothing which are found too difficult to make can always be ordered to specification.

Making Costumes.—For those who decide to make their own costumes the following hints are humbly offered. Use pure colours ; choose your material for its " hang " as well as its appearance ; remember that vertical lines accentuate height, horizontal lines breadth ; aim at sweeping effects ; exaggerate the outlines of your design (patterns for fancy dress will *not* be appropriate for the stage), and use the historical treatises on the subject for suggestion and inspiration only. Subjugate the historical to the decorative and symbolic. To quote Komisarjevsky once again : " The naturalistic and genuine historical costume, since it is never an expression of the manner in which any artistic play is written, or of the individual understanding of a play by any artist-producer, is quite useless on the stage. . . . A magnificent dress taken direct from a

---

[1] Unless they are very conventionalized. Egyptian ones (*e.g.* for *Cæsar and Cleopatra*) can be made of black wool, with dozens of tiny plaits.

museum on to the stage means nothing. An actor dressed in a genuine historical costume on a stage cannot look anything other than a museum piece of a waxwork from Madame Tussaud's."

Materials.—Coarse materials—Bolton sheeting, unbleached calico, hessian—often yield surprisingly good results when dyed or when stencilled with oils ; coloured blankets stencilled make excellent cloaks ; furnishing remnants (especially the cheaper velvets) often come in handy. Sateens and artificial silks reflect light well, but do not stand up to wear. Butter muslin (about 2½d. a yard) has a surprising variety of stage uses—especially for revue items (the heliotrope colour will take all light-colours perfectly) ; tinsel gauze (in silver or gold) can be rather amusing. Scout scarves can be most useful, both as head-gear and waist-gear, and under coloured light can look quite beautiful. Artificial crêpe de Chine takes light well ; real crêpe de Chine, of course, is better, but expensive (from 5s. 11d. a yard).

Hand properties—except in fantasy—ought to be convincing ; wooden swords or papier-mâché pewter tankards only annoy the audience. Armour should neither be " all steel " nor all dishcloth and cardboard ; it should clank in moderation. String knitted on thick wooden needles has more body than dishcloth ; a suggestion of aluminium paint is more convincing than a mass attack. Armour gauntlets can be made, by those who have the knack, by attaching little pieces of cardboard to a basis of old glove. Sandals can be carved from old slippers or tennis shoes, and—if required—the tapes carried cross-gartered to the knee. Helmets can be constructed, with the help of glue and hessian and considerable faith, from the crowns of old felt or bowler hats. Hats, incidentally, should not be worn if it can be avoided (except to conceal the absence of wigs), unless fairly strong footlights are used. One of our ladies once aged about thirty years at the dress rehearsal because the proscenium spots cast the shadow of her hat brim over her face.　There was a hectic search for a hat of less obstructive fashion !

Tights usually look fairly ghastly—particularly the cotton ones which most amateurs are obliged, for economy's sake, to use.　There is more chance of avoiding unsightly wrinkles if the garments are washed in lux and warm water before *every* occasion on which they are to be worn.　Once a week is worse than useless.

Fans and banners should be made a definite part of the decorative scheme.

Costume and Lighting.—The effect of stage lighting upon costume-colours has already been mentioned.　Materials which look rich and vivid in the shop often look washed out or dingy on the stage.　This is less likely to happen if the white light of the stage is made by combining several colours ; each dress then seems to reflect its appropriate colour.　Coloured light falling on costumes may be a nuisance—or it may be an asset. If a girl in a blue dress moves into the area of an amber spotlight, it will be a nuisance—the dress will appear dirty green, and the spotlight may have to be changed to rose.[1]　But, on the other hand, characters may be emphasized by a light falling upon them which brings out to the full the richness of their costume.　And such emphasis may be varied.　Subtle changes of lighting-colour may transfer interest from one character to another, emphasizing domination or submission. This may be done by spotlighting (two spotlights of different colours trained on a character and the colour proportions varied), or even by changes in the general lighting.　Even the character of the dress can be made to appear to change.　As an extreme example, witness the effects you can obtain in a revue number by dressing a chorus in red and green, and light-

---

[1] It is useful to experiment with actual samples of dress material under different coloured lights on the model stage.

ing them first with the one colour, then the other. As a more serious example, a device which we used in the last Act of *R.U.R.* may be instanced. The Act symbolizes the dawn of the sense of beauty and love in the minds of the Robots. At the end of it, it is essential that Helena the Robotess should appear almost transcendentally radiant. Yet when she first steals into the darkened laboratory one wants to avoid the suggestion that she is clad in some kind of nightdress or party frock. She was therefore dressed in light cream silk stuff covered with smoke-grey silk net. At first she appeared an almost ghostly figure, then, as the day dawned and the light grew in intensity, her dress grew more lively, and finally, when she passed into the rays of the sun, all suggestion of greyness disappeared. (See Frontispiece.)

Costume and the Players.—Costume should be " practicable "—it should help the actor in his movements, not encumber him. And he in his turn should learn to make the most of its possibilities—to utilize, for instance, both the decorative and the dramatic qualities of drapery. Irving, who said that " the right thing " upon the stage was " at once the most effective and the most becoming," used to wear his costumes a considerable time before the date of performance, and he related of Macready that in his efforts to make himself feel at home as Henry V. he even went to bed in his armour ! Boys, then, should have experience of their costumes (not merely upon the stage) well before the show. The hang of a costume, of course, owes much to the way it is put on, and (especially with a " lady ") to the garments worn underneath.

COSTUMIERS

Charles Fox, Ltd., 72 Long Acre, W.C.2.
H. and M. Rayne, Ltd., 15 Rupert Street, W.1.

B. J. Simmons and Co., Ltd., 7 King Street, Covent Garden, W.C.2.

D. and J. Benjamin, 3–9 Hanway Street, Oxford Street, W.1.

And various provincial firms, such as Drury's of Brighton and Birkenshaws of Liverpool.

The British Drama League (incorporating the Village Drama Society), 8 Adelphi Terrace, W.C.2, has a useful collection of costumes which can be borrowed quite reasonably.

Costumes can also be had from Citizen House, Bath.

PERRUQUIERS

Gustave, 1 Long Acre, W.C.2.

Clarksons, 41–44 Wardour St., W.1.

Spaans, 7 Lisle Street, W.C.2.

Note.—Before orders are sent for either costumes or wigs, the appropriate measurement forms should be obtained. It is sometimes worth the additional expense to have hired wigs " dressed " by some first-class local hairdresser.

PLATE XVII.—Lino-cut advertising
stamp for envelopes.
(*See page* 146.)

CHAPTER IX.—THE BUSINESS SIDE

1. Organizing for a Performance

Permission and Royalties.—Before any modern play can be legally performed in public, permission must be sought from the author's agents or the owners of the copyright. (Copyright covers the period of the author's life and fifty years after his death.) Clearly, this permission should be sought before the play is put into rehearsal, because it is not always forthcoming. (Permission to perform Savoy opera, for example, may depend upon the touring plans of the D'Oyly Carte Company.)

The royalty, which is payable a few days in advance, may vary from 10s. 6d. for a one-act play to £5, 5s. for a full-length play—with a slight concession for performances after the first. For Savoy opera, in addition to the royalty, a deposit of £20 is necessary to secure the band parts. Some dramatists will accept royalties on a percentage basis, which is a great help to the small society. The payment of the royalty should be a matter of honour, for, as Mr. John Hampden points out, it is in many cases the chief source of the dramatist's income, and is simply a payment for the right to use his property. " A dramatist," he says, " should never be asked to waive his royalty because the performance is in aid of charity, for he prefers to choose for himself the charities to which he is to contribute. (Such performances are good for charity and bad for amateur drama ; they suggest that the latter is not on its own account worth paying to see.)"

Publicity.—While "box office" is not the aim of school dramatics, the larger the attendance the larger the financial surplus for future development. Besides, it is more pleasing to play to "full" houses. [1] The sale of tickets can be helped in various ways.

(*a*) *Internal.*—(1) In the preceding issue of the magazine an account may be given of the forthcoming production. This account may be reproduced as a leaflet at very small extra charge if the type has not been broken up. (2) A roneo-d circular may be sent to parents describing the forthcoming performances, and inviting their patronage. (3) A special advertising stamp, lino-cut in the Art Room (make sure that it is artistic), may be attached to all envelopes bearing school communications (Plate XVII.). (4) A poster campaign, organized by the Art Department, may stimulate interest amongst the boys. (5) (Most effective of all if you stoop to it !) Complimentary tickets may be given to boys who take orders for tickets amounting to a certain value.

(*b*) *Press.*—In a small town there will be little difficulty in securing "advance publicity" in the local press ; almost any material submitted will be accepted. In a city, however, you may have to compete for space with news of national importance, and if you want publicity more subtle methods can be adopted. "Pars," suited in style to their intended medium, can be fired in to the various "feature" columns of the paper— to the gossip columns, to the women's page (on the costume, or the *décor*, for instance)—as well as to the amateur dramatic columns and the news pages proper. (Different readers read different sections of the paper ; a single item is easily overlooked.) Photographers may be invited a fortnight or so before the show to record the making or painting of scenery,

---

[1] Simonson points out how "inhibited" audiences are in a half-empty theatre. "The explosive force of an audience's emotion, like that of powder in a cartridge, depends very largely on how tight the audience is packed" (page 30).

and again on the day of dress rehearsal. Complimentary
tickets should be sent well in advance, and programmes as
soon as they are ready.

Sale of Tickets.—A Bookings Manager should be appointed
to look after the organization and sale of tickets ; he will have
no light job. Tickets should be printed as artistically as
possible, and contain no more words than are necessary. (If
you decide to exclude late-comers during the overture, as you
should, this should be stated on the ticket.) The tickets may
be of various colours for different nights and prices. (Ask the
Handicraft Room to make a cabinet to accommodate them !)
Plans of the seating will be necessary. (Colour them to match
the tickets.) Cloakroom tickets can be used for numbering
seats. It will afford more people a good view of the stage (and
ease your problem of sight lines) if you arrange the hall with
two side gangways than if you use one centre gangway.
Emergency exits should be clearly labelled. For all notices
the lettering should be good, and the help of the Art Department might be evoked. The Bookings Manager should also
be responsible for Stewards and Programme Sellers.

If boys are allowed to take bundles of tickets to sell it will
be necessary to print far more than can actually be sold ; daily
returns of such sellings should be taken to prevent possible over-
selling. Reserved tickets can have a space left blank upon
them for the seat number, and when a boy sells such a ticket
he can bring it in and have a number filled in according to his
choosing on the plan.

The Programme.—The programme is an introduction to
the play, and should be in keeping with it. The printing
should be attractive and artistic—that is, as simple as possible.
The printers who submit the lowest estimates too often love
to embellish their handiwork with flourishes ; it is wise to
specify the spacing and the sizes of type, and to insist on seeing
proofs. Some study of the relative suitability of various

FIG. 30.—Lino cut for programme by Bert Brown.

founts of type and kinds of printing paper to various sorts of play may be found amusing, and it is fun to explore the typographical resources of the locality. The design of a cover-block may provide further exercise for the Art Department. Fig. 30 shows a design executed by a fifteen-year-old boy.

The programme should nominate the cast in the order of entrance. It helps the " team feeling," though it may be of little use to the audience, if the names of stage hands and switchboard assistants are also printed. Announcements of the light-hearted numbers in a revue should be in key—in the spirit, say, of the Co-Optimists' programmes. A phrase may often indicate to the audience the mood in which an item should be approached (*e.g. The Discovery—a study of Idealism* versus *the Mob*—by Herman Ould). For full-length works the programme may well contain (perhaps on an inserted leaf) a note on the character of the play, or, if it is an opera, a synopsis of the plot (written in an appropriately mock-heroic vein if it is Savoy opera !). An example " from actual play " may be quoted. (See page 150.)

Finance.—The Treasurer may be assisted by a Finance and General Purposes Committee, consisting of the Headmaster, the Producer, the Scenic Manager, the Electrician, and any other " Heads of Departments."

Sitting as a Committee of Ways and Means, they may review the balance from the previous year, and estimate probable receipts, deciding on the price of seats, etc. As a Committee of Supply they may examine the estimates prepared by the Spending Departments of their requirements for the forthcoming show, and authorize expenditure up to a certain amount. (The Treasurer should see that these estimates are not exceeded without further authorization.) They will decide what margin remains for " Capital expansion " (permanent equipment, *e.g.* curtains). After the show a Cash Statement should be prepared, and then every item of ex-

THE THEME OF THE PLAY
Man *versus* Machines

The theme of the play is the revolt of the Robots, which Man, out of his ingenuity, has devised.

What exactly are these Robots ? Unfortunately, the pandering to sensation in the original London production, combined with the adoption of the word to describe a common mechanical device, has given the public a conception of a Robot as a kind of armour-plated automaton. This is not Capek's conception. He gives us no actual description of them, but it is clear from the text that, although manufactured industrially, the Robots are made like human beings, with the same kind of skin and flesh and bones. Our production is true to that conception.

What Capek has done is to suggest that these creatures are analogous to machines, in the sense that Mankind who creates them cannot control them. The machines, instead of being the slaves, become the taskmasters. Instead of setting Man free for the pursuit of the things he cherishes, they confine him to attending upon their wants, and impose on him new sets of values. He is in their grip.

At times in the play Capek clearly identifies his Robots with the industrial working classes. It may be that he wishes to suggest that machines, as a modern thinker has put it, " tend to impose something of their nature upon those who serve them, their uniformity, their regularity, their soullessness." It is really " machine mentality " that Capek is satirizing, and we try to bring this out, in the present production, in ways that are, we think, original. But this satire of industrial conditions is rather gratuitous ; it is no integral part of the main theme, and it would be quite wrong (as the author has agreed) to see in the revolt of the Robots any revolt of the Masses.

The central problem of the play impinges on most of the great social and economic questions of the times—unemployment, " over-production," our new friend " technocracy," even the export of arms to the Far East. And, surveying the world, one may well ask, " Has Man, in embracing mechanical ' progress ' without weighing the social consequences or striving for a comparable advance in ethics, brought upon himself destruction ? "

Overleaf you will find Capek's own comment upon it all.

The Epilogue takes us out of economics into poetry : in this new chapter of Genesis it is the elemental uncontaminated desires of the human mind—for love, for beauty—that offer hope for the future.

Overleaf was printed an extract from a very illuminating article which Capek wrote in *The Saturday Review* when his play first aroused controversy in London.

penditure should be scrutinized to ascertain to what extent it was " current " or " capital," so that the actual cost of staging the particular show can be worked out (*e.g.* royalties and scene-paint would be " current " ; sashlines or proscenium borders would be regarded as " capital " ; flats or screens for which there would be further use might be accounted partly to each). This Committee should be responsible for working the Five Year Plan.

A Five Year Plan.—Schools need never be daunted by the cost of equipment. At the outset it is usually possible to borrow. Local amateur societies, the professional theatres, and electrical firms are usually quite willing to help with the loan of curtains, floodlights, and spotlights. Even a switch-board can be hired cheaply (only don't hire an electrician with it if you can help it !). With a platform, a few overhead lights, and some courage, any school can face the public. But as its resources grow it should improve its equipment in accord-ance with a carefully thought out plan. Here is a possible five year programme :

Overhead compartment lights.
Provisional switchboard.
Platform extension.
Front curtains and pelmet.
Back-cloth.
Compartment lights for back-cloth.
False proscenium—flats and border.
Floodlights (home-made).
Dimmers (liquid, home-made ; metallic, purchased).
Metallic frames (for gelatine) for all compartment lights.
Switchboard—extend.
Back draperies.
Traverse curtain.
Spotlights.
Rail track for curtains.

Second set back draperies, if first non-reversible.
Trough for footlights.
Stage floor-cloth.
Floodlights—purchased.
Permanent " point " wiring and plug sockets.

The order of purchase and manufacture will depend on what can be borrowed and the type of shows given.

At the same time a programme for scenery in the narrower sense should be drawn up.   At the end of five years, in addition to the permanent equipment listed above, the society should possess a complete set of unit flats and a fair assortment of three-dimensional units.   (A catalogue of Hall's equipment, and price lists from electrical firms and manufacturers of canvas and other accessories—*e.g.* McDougall's—should be obtained at the outset.)

In the writer's school of five hundred boys in a depressed industrial city the average " takings " (with the highest priced seats at 2s.) exceed £100 a year.   For the three performances of *The Mikado* the takings were nearly £130.   This is a new school, with no " Old Boys' Society " to swell its audiences.   On a basis of this kind a plan such as is outlined above is by no means fantastic.

2. *Some Legal Points*

Probably most school societies break the law in some way or other, but then it is clear that their activities were not always envisaged when the law was made, and authority is wisely slow to intervene.   If official ruling is deliberately sought, it will be found to be somewhat as follows :

Licence of Buildings.—Buildings are required to be licensed for " public performances of stage plays " (maximum penalty, £20 for each day of offence).   It is a public performance if the

public are invited, whether there is any admission charge or
not. Permanent licences carry elaborate rules, and heavy
financial sureties are demanded. An *occasional licence* can be
obtained from the local authority (usually the County or
Borough Council, in some cases the Licensing Justices) for a
nominal fee. It is granted to the owner or responsible manager
of the premises, *not* to the promoter of the play, and is
valid only on the days or during the period for which it is
granted.

Licensing of Plays.—If schools produce new plays for the
first time in public, it would seem that they must have them
licensed by the Lord Chamberlain, whose reading fees range
from £1, 1s. to £2, 2s., according to the number of acts and
scenes. (Apply to The Comptroller, Lord Chamberlain's
Office, St. James's Palace.) This requirement applies to all
" stage plays " (the legal definition of which is wide enough
to cover almost any form of entertainment—including even
" mime " plays), and to additions to already licensed plays,
which are performed " for hire " (which means that a charge is
made for admission, not that the actors are paid) at " any
theatre." (*Question*. Is a hall licensed for occasional performances legally a " theatre " ?) It will not apply to *bona fide
private* performances.

Entertainments Tax.—Exemption from tax can be claimed :

(*a*) For School Entertainments.

A declaration is necessary " that the entertainment will
be provided solely for the purpose of promoting some object
in connection with the school," and " that all persons taking
part as performers will be persons who are receiving, or have
received, instruction in the school," and, furthermore, " that
the school is not conducted or established for profit." A
similar exemption covers certain educational organizations
providing " social and physical training " for children and
juveniles.

Apply for Form E.D.23 to the local Customs and Excise Office, and send it at least fourteen days before the date of the entertainment to the Commissioners of Customs and Excise, Custom House, E.C.3.

(*b*) For Entertainments of a Wholly Educational Character.

Application should be made by letter, giving all particulars direct to the Commissioners at Custom House. There is a right of appeal to the Board of Education in the case of a difference of opinion. At least a fortnight's notice is necessary ; obviously, more is desirable.

(*c*) For Entertainments " Partly Educational."

Exemption may be sought where the entertainment is provided for " partly educational or partly scientific purposes by a Society, Institution, or Committee, not conducted or established for profit," or by an organization with the object of " reviving national pastimes." Apply as in the case of (*b*).

(*d*) For Entertainments on behalf of Charities.

There are various forms of exemption under this head, all of them designed to ensure that the cause of charity is not put forward merely as an excuse for exemption. Except in the case of old established societies, it is required, either that *all* the takings be handed over without any charge for expenses, or that the *net* proceeds be handed over, provided the expenses do not amount to 50 per cent. of the receipts. For details, apply to the local Customs Office, or see Stuart Page's book, *The Law of the Amateur Stage.*

CHAPTER X.—THE MODEL STAGE AND THE STAGE-CRAFT GUILD

SEVERAL references have been made already to the use of a model stage. The subject is important enough to deserve a chapter of its own.

The model stage must not be dismissed as a mere toy; the most serious artists of the theatre use it. Craig's projected National School for the Theatre was to consist largely, it will be remembered, of series of detailed models of settings for standard plays, each play being represented by several series illustrating various possible methods of interpretation and presentation. For school purposes the model has special value.

The Uses of the Model.—(1) The first use of a model is to enable the producer to make his ideas clear to those who will have to execute them. When Craig confronted Stanislavsky with his typically vague designs for *Hamlet*, Stanislavsky had a large model of his stage constructed with a lighting set corresponding exactly to that possessed by the theatre, and in the model everything was worked out to the minutest detail. The school producer who knows nothing of stage carpentry or practical electricity can work out his ideas on the model, and then approach the departmental experts with some hope of making clear to them what he wants done.

(2) This will suggest the private value of a model to the producer. He can " try out " various arrangements of his scenic units, flat and three-dimensional. With the help of the simple lighting model described below he can experiment with

the placing of lights to obtain various effects. He can observe the decorative value of light and shade. He can study the principles of colour harmony and combination. Actual changes of light from one colour to another can be carried through the whole range of intermediate tones, and the effect upon the colours of scenery or upon shadows cast by objects, no less than the psychological value of the various hues and their appropriateness to various scenes of plays, can be learned by demonstration.

(3) The value of such an instrument does not stop with the producer. It can be used to open new worlds of beauty to the pupil in the school. It can help enormously to heighten imaginative appreciation of dramatic literature. Boys can be encouraged to design " sets " which convey the atmosphere of particular scenes, and to devise appropriate lighting for them. Show them some illustrations of strikingly effective stage designs by the great masters, let them re-create a scene or two, perhaps, from such examples, and then challenge them to make something original.

After all, there is nothing esoteric or supernatural about stage designing. As Milton Smith says : " The steps are few and simple, and they can even be taught to children : (1) try to find the theme or central idea of the play ; (2) note two or three colours as being the key colours, suggested by the play ; (3) feel what sort of lines will be most appropriate—long, sweeping lines, or short and jolly ones ; and (4) try to express your ideas by drawings, or, better still, by a stage model of the set and sketches for the costumes." Incidentally, children who are unable to express themselves with pencil or brush may find a source of real creative joy in dimmer controls and gelatine filters.

Scenes so designed can be used most effectively in class. You show to the class a model of a scene—say, the courtyard of Macbeth's castle, or the " blasted heath," or the wall of

Troy—made really luminous and *alive* by light (and you must see the beauty of coloured light on a model stage before you will believe what amazing effects are possible), and then, when the right atmosphere has been obtained, the scene can be read through.[1] For this purpose a darkened room is usually necessary; the characters can read their parts with the aid of concealed flash-lamps. Designs should be broad and sweeping in their effect; mood matters more than accuracy of detail; and the purpose is to release, not to limit imagination.

Such activities can well be linked up with the normal work in Art. Appreciation of the essential qualities in composition and design can be fostered. Other developments of the idea will suggest themselves. By the possession of a model stage, a school can multiply enormously the opportunities of its pupils to experience the full spiritual powers of drama.

A New Classroom Method.—The model stage is particularly useful to enlist the interest of the non-literary type of scholar. From it, indeed, is developing a new classroom approach to dramatic literature. A class has read, say, a ballad or a scene from a play, and naturally clamours to be allowed to act it. Remembering that the school hall is occupied at the moment, and that the floor of your classroom has to act as the non-soundproof ceiling of the classroom underneath, you point out to the boys that before a play can be acted some one has to think out all the movements of the actors, and to plan the action generally. You explain to them what " producing a play " means. And then you ask each boy to imagine that he is called upon to produce the play or scene in question, and to make his plan accordingly. You suggest that they regard the desk-top as the stage platform, and that they move their characters about upon it as they think necessary. Little

[1] This plan of reading the play through was used with the Moscow model, and Stanislavsky describes how, in these experiments, the text of *Hamlet* came to take on new meaning for him.

pieces of paper, bent so as to stand upright, and labelled, can serve as characters, or chessmen can be used. Soon you will find boys making more permanent figures of card or wood in their spare time, and perhaps devising interesting units to stand, say, for groups in crowd scenes. Scenery is unnecessary, though a few cut-outs for trees, etc., may be useful. Different stage levels and steps can be built up simply with the help of books.

You have only to watch a class busily working (or playing, if you like) in this way, to realize that the method enables the printed words to live for many to whom otherwise they would be dead, and that it serves to develop in all that capacity to visualize action and movement that lies at the heart of enjoyable play-reading. Incidentally, you will soon find some of your " non-literary " boys coming along to ask if they may " make their own plays."

A Stage-craft Guild.—In the writer's school one branch of the Dramatic Society is known as the Stage-craft Guild. It consists of those interested in the technical and æsthetic aspects of staging and lighting. Some folios of scene design and lighting (such as the books of Cheney, and Selden and Sellman) are available for the members, and occasional lectures are given on these subjects illustrated with epidiascope projections and demonstrations on the model stage. Occasional exhibitions are held of the members' own models. In addition, the members pay occasional visits to the stages of the local commercial and repertory theatres, where they see various types of stage appliance, and where the management usually arrange a special demonstration of stage lighting in their honour.

From the members of the Guild, as far as possible, the stage and electrical assistants for the school shows are chosen. Some of the members now possess sufficient technical experience to be entrusted, say, with the job of converting a general description of lighting requirements to a definite light plot ;

and of devising the colour schemes for those revue items
(*e.g.* burlesque dance troupes) in which the rare indulgence of
" lighting for lighting's sake " is permissible.

If it be true, as Mr. Norman Marshall says, that " the crying
need of the English theatre at the moment is for theatrically
educated audiences, audiences who have some theoretical
knowledge of the various branches of the art of the theatre,"
then this work may conceivably be of some value.   Musicians,
painters, and authors, he says, can rely on at least a reasonable

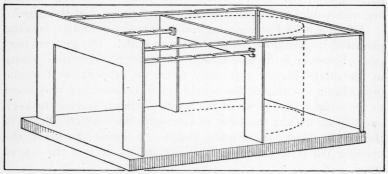

Fig. 31.—Framework of model stage.

proportion of their audience having some technical appreciation
of music, painting, and writing.   " Even elementary school
children are now taught the rudiments of an intelligent appreciation of these arts, but intelligent appreciation of the art
of the theatre has, as yet, hardly begun to exist." [1]

Construction of a Model.—A model stage can be built in a
variety of ways.   Fig. 31 shows the skeleton framework—and a
skeleton is all that is needed—of a model that has proved quite
successful in practice.   The base is made in the form of a box
into which the various units can be packed when dismantled.

[1] Preface to Ridge, *Stage Lighting*.

(Care should be taken that the panel used for the base is not warped, or there may be difficulty in persuading scenery to stand upright on it.)   H. W. Wanslow, in *Everybody's Theatre*, gives exceedingly full instructions for making a puppet theatre which could easily be employed for the purposes here outlined. As for size, satisfactory lighting by means of pocket-lamp bulbs, as described on page 163, will be impossible if the model is too large.   That shown in Fig. 31 is 20 inches wide, corresponding to the 40 feet of the school hall ; the " back-cloths " used are of half-imperial size drawing-paper, the lower set of rails (which are removable) being inserted to carry " drops " of this size.

When a model of a setting for an actual production is being prepared it should be made strictly to scale.   For general purposes, however, it may be wise to have the proscenium opening in the model bigger, especially taller, in proportion than the proscenium opening of the school stage, because one may want to see what is going on in the model without having to keep one's head within the limit of the sight lines which obtain in the big building ; it is quite simple, of course, to mask the opening till it is exactly proportionate to that of the school stage.

Similarly, to aid lighting effects, it is advisable to leave more depth in proportion than you are likely to have on your real stage.   The " back-cloth " can be pinned on to the back-piece shown, or hung, pinned to a batten of strip-wood, just in front of it.

Better still, a piece of white cardboard bent into a curve (as shown by the dotted lines) can be used as a cyclorama dome.   The liveliness and luminosity of coloured light reflected from such a background is astounding.   The eye cannot focus upon its surface, and the spectator seems to gaze into space of infinite depth and richness.

On this model " drop-scenes " of plain paper can be used— white or pale grey or blue for a sky-cloth (if there is no cyclo-

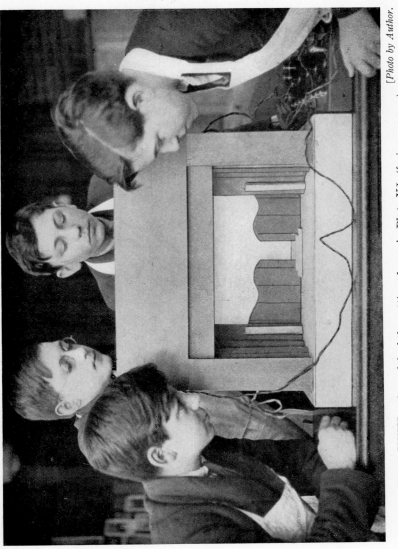

[*Photo by Author.*

PLATE XVIII.—A model of the setting shown in Plate XI. (facing page 92).

rama), grey or black to represent a curtain background. (Curtains of stuff seldom hang well enough to be used on a model.) Drop-scenes not in use can be hung in the rear part of the model. Painted back-scenes on the real stage we condemned ; on the model, however, by a skilful use of colours for your paints (water-colours) and lights you can make the various planes stand out so that you could swear you could pass your hand between the foreground and the far distance. The painted " ground-row " with the plain sky-cloth behind is, of course, even more effective.

One effect, not corresponding to anything practicable on a school stage but well worth trying on the model for its own sake, is the lighting of the back-cloth from behind. Try a dawn effect, lighting your paper back-cloth at the back first with a dim blue at the base, so that your landscape (which must be blacked out on the back of the sheet with Indian ink if it is painted on the back-cloth direct) stands out in silhouette ; then flood in a little rose, adding at the same time some blue above. Gradually work in blue overhead *in front,* and then amber to pick out the landscape. The sense of distance and atmosphere you get is incredible.

Another experiment is to place a cardboard cut-out (say of a castle, though any piece of interesting form will serve) upon the stage and arrange lights of various colours at varying positions from it, so that they throw grotesque shadows upon the back-cloth. By varying the intensity of the lights a symphony of changing form and colour can be played ; again, it has to be seen to be believed. Its practical value is in demonstrating colour mixture and the colour value of shadows.

Scenic units will consist of (*a*) blocks and steps and platforms, made of solid wood, on the unit principle described in previous chapters ; (*b*) " flats "—on the same principle— made of stout cardboard or ply-wood. They can be made to stand upright by means of small wooden blocks fixed at the base, or they can be joined (as in Fig. 32 A) by a steel wire passing through hinges of gummed paper. "Flats" so joined

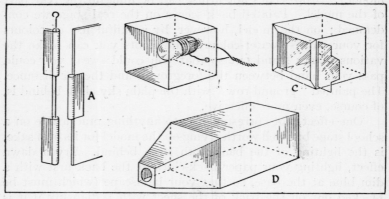

FIG. 32.

will show light through the cracks, and therefore (*c*) suitable scenes, such as interiors, can be cut out of a single piece of card and bent to stand erect. Selden and Sellman describe in some detail how to do this, and Smith devotes several chapters to it. You can, of course, introduce endless refinements. Your pupils soon will, any way!

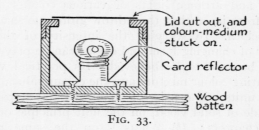

Lid cut out, and colour-medium stuck on.

Card reflector

Wood batten

FIG. 33.

The Lighting Equipment.—Far and away the most important part of the stage model is the lighting equipment. Ordinary

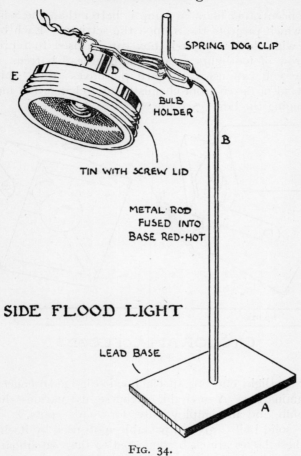

SPRING DOG CLIP

E   D

BULB
HOLDER

B

TIN WITH SCREW LID

METAL ROD
FUSED INTO
BASE RED-HOT

SIDE FLOOD LIGHT

LEAD BASE

A

FIG. 34.

pocket-lamp bulbs are used, each one placed in a miniature
flood-box of cardboard about an inch cube in size (Fig. 32 B)
provided with a lid (Fig. 32 C) in which can be inserted a slide
of coloured gelatine, of the type used on the stage proper.

(The concentrated filament lamp is better than the S-filament lamp, which projects the S upon the setting.)　Each box will give a wide flood; a single box can be used to represent a whole row of footlights or a whole overhead batten.　(Alternatively you can use cardboard pill-boxes—the "chipette" type at 5d. a dozen from chemists—and change the mediums by changing the lids.　See Fig. 33.)

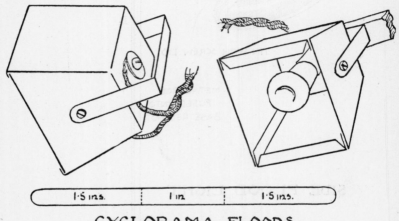

1·5 ins.　　1 in.　　1·5 ins.

CYCLORAMA FLOODS
FIG. 35.

For spotlight effects a special hood (Fig. 32 D) concentrates the illumination.　You could, of course, use various shapes of small bulb, and also employ lenses for your "spots."　The so-called "solid bulb" gives a passable spot, used by itself.

If these boxes are each connected to the switchboard by a yard or so of thin flex, they can be used in any position in the wings, or on the stage floor, or hung on rods or thin laths overhead (hence the grooves in the rails), or hooked to the proscenium.　Some of them can, of course, be wired in permanent positions.

Figs. 34 and 35 show some metal light-boxes devised by a boy owner of a model stage.

The switchboard, which can be as big as you please, is quite simply constructed. The one illustrated (Fig. 36) has five circuits, and costs 14s., including the ebonite. The terminals, XY, are linked either to a 4-volt accumulator or to a trans-

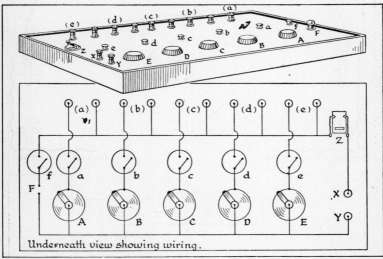

FIG. 36.—A model switchboard.

former plugged to the A.C. mains.[1] Z is a main cut-out switch. A, B, C, D, E are dimmers (30 ohm radio rheostats bought for a few pence each) ; a, b, c, d, e are cut-out switches ; and (a), (b), (c), (d), (e) the terminals to which the lamps are connected. F is a pilot lamp controlled by a switch at f. You can attach single lamps to each circuit, or link, say, a series of red lamps

[1] Be sure it is alternating current, not direct. The amperage of the transformer should be adequate to allow the required number of bulbs to be lit without the switching on of any of them diminishing the power of the others.

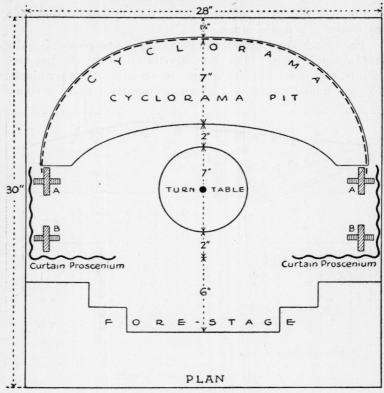

FIG. 37.—Plan of model stage.

to (a), of green lamps to (b), and so on. The unit can be
extended indefinitely, and master dimmers can be introduced
if desired.

Another Model

The second model illustrated (Figs. 37–41), which has been
designed by Mr. M. V. C. Jeffreys, is based more upon the

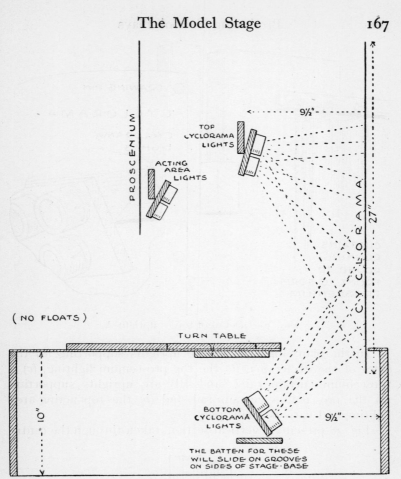

Fig. 38.—Vertical section.

ideal than upon the actual theatre. Less adaptable than that just described, it is capable of greater imaginative effect, and for use as an aid to theatric appreciation would be an asset to any school.

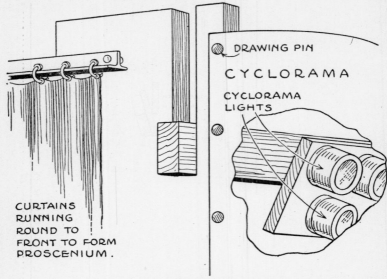

CURTAINS
RUNNING
ROUND TO
FRONT TO FORM
PROSCENIUM.

DRAWING PIN

CYCLORAMA

CYCLORAMA
LIGHTS

Fig. 39.—Detail of top of upright A.

In the plan (Fig. 37) AA are uprights supporting (*a*) the sides of the cyclorama, (*b*) the top proscenium lighting, (*c*) a proscenium curtain rail; and BB are uprights supporting (*a*) the proscenium curtain rail and (*b*) the top acting-area lighting and various small spots.

Fig. 38 presents a vertical section, taken through the centre

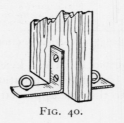

Fig. 40.

from front to back. Fig. 39 shows a detail of the top of upright
A, with the cyclorama cut away to show the lighting batten.
This batten slots into the uprights, and bridges the top of the
stage.

Figs. 40 and 41 show details of construction. Fig. 40 shows
the method of fastening the uprights AA and BB to the stage
floor, and Fig. 41 shows how the corners of the main stage may
be constructed to avoid mortising or halving; the sides (of
board 10 inch by ½ inch) are simply screwed at the corners to
posts (2 inch by 2 inch by 10 inch).

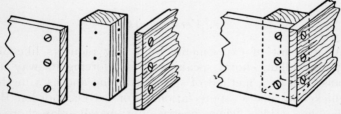

FIG. 41.—Detail showing construction of corners of main stage-base.

CHAPTER XI.—THE CLASSROOM AND THE STAGE

THERE are various ways in which the ordinary work of the school can be made to contribute ideas to a general dramatic entertainment of the kind described on page 13, Chapter I.

1. Verse Choirs

As a result of experiments by a few pioneers like Miss Marjorie Gullan, choral speaking is fast forcing its way into schools both as a method of speech training and as a method of quickening poetic appreciation. For, as Dr. Gordon Bottomley has said, " when poetry—not merely play-choruses, but any poetry with a choric quality—is thoroughly rehearsed by a band of trained speakers under the leadership of one of them, something of a different (and a valuable) nature is heard to have come into existence. A body of lovely tone is attained that cannot be attained in any other way ; expressiveness is enhanced, carrying power and intelligibility are ever magnified, and the native rhythms of the poem make their effect in a way that they cannot do when underlined—and too often masked— by musical composition." Those who are unfamiliar with the method should consult the admirable books of Miss Gullan (see Bibliography, p. 195).

When a reasonable standard of artistic expression is reached, such choirs can " perform " acceptably in public. An experiment made by the writer in staging a choric rendering of Masefield's *Cargoes* may suggest possibilities still unexplored. The

poem had been prepared on the lines suggested by Miss Gullan ;
a form was divided into three groups, each group taking
a stanza, light voices being chosen for the first stanza, rich
" dark " voices for the second, and voices with vigour and
" edge " for the third. The first verse was delivered slowly,
with an almost sensuous lingering over the sounds ; the second
had something more robust about it, but it was still a dream
picture ; in the third verse romance gave way to hard reality,
the smooth rhythm of " rowing home to haven " changed
abruptly to the broken effect of " butting through the Channel,"
the music of vowels was submerged in the clash of consonants—
everything was staccato, and the conductor whipped up the
tempo almost to a fury in the last few lines. The poem was
delivered against a setting of black velvet. The proscenium
curtains opened to show a stage in utter darkness. Then a
spotlight (amber) welled up and revealed to one side of the
stage the group who were to say the first verse. After the
verse the spotlight faded, the members of the group silently
removed themselves behind the curtains, and another spot
(rose colour) came up to reveal the second group to the other
side of the stage. Both these spots were so placed as to throw
no harsh shadows. For the third verse the remaining group
(central) were lit by a horizontal beam of hard white light
switched on suddenly from the wing ; at the end of line 1 it
was switched off, and another spot came on simultaneously
from the other wing ; the two spots were reversed again at
the end of lines 2 and 3, and then on each of the remaining six
beats, accelerating in time with the conductor, and ending in
a black-out. These shifting searchlights gave an impression
of urgency, bustle, modern restlessness, and materialism—
similar to the effect produced in the final scene of *Cavalcade*.
Some may exclaim " sacrilege ! " others may recognize a
perfectly reverent method of reinforcing the emotional appeals
of the verse. The use of costume, it may be thought, might

have helped also, but the verses are so short that they would
have been over before the audience had diverted its attention
from the clothes to the words.   Costume would be appropriate
if it could be used so that, like the lightning, it served to induce
in the audience an appropriate mood without distracting by
an intrinsic decorative appeal.

2. Ballads

Every teacher of English knows the fun of dramatizing ballads in the classroom.   Dramatizations of ballads are also worth
considering for public performance, and in their presentation
it should be possible to attain a high level of artistic excellence.
The Children's Theatre productions have shown what genuine
beauty may be achieved by the simplest of means.

In the writer's experience there are three types or stages
of ballad presentation.   (1) The first is in the classroom, where
dramatization is part of the normal course of events ;   (2) the
second is in the school hall on the last afternoon of term, or
some similar occasion when selected ballads are played to an
audience of the whole school ;   (3) the third is the public
presentation when, as part of a programme of one-act plays
and other odds and ends, ballads are performed in appropriate
settings, reinforced by the fullest resources of stage lighting.

The first stage will be largely spontaneous.   The players
will read from their books ;   there will be no special costumes ;
properties and places will be imagined.   The teacher may,
perhaps, intervene to point out opportunities for miming which
the players are missing.   The second stage will be played in a
curtain setting—at any rate with some proscenium wings and
a traverse curtain—with full dress and perhaps properties of
sorts, and for this the players must learn their parts.   But there
will still be a large measure of spontaneity ;   indeed it may be a

joyous "rag." The third stage will need careful arrangement and rehearsal.

Preliminary Planning.—I have said that the first stage will be largely spontaneous, and so far as the actual playing goes that is true enough. But the mechanics of the action must have been planned first. The teacher would do well to envisage the final presentation of stage three before he goes into the class. He must decide the scenes into which the ballad must be split up, what lines are to be allotted to the " chorus," what spoken by the players and what omitted, and where the various players are to enter and leave. A few slight verbal modifications (*e.g.* to avoid awkward " said he's ") may be necessary ; the repetition of a phrase will usually repair the broken rhythm. (After a little practice the pupils can be asked to make their own " acting versions," and it is a profitable exercise to discuss these, their merits and shortcomings, in class.)

There are various ways of procedure. One of the methods adopted by the writer is to draw upon the board a ground-plan of the stage, with the various entrances numbered. This plan enables the pupils to imagine that the front of the classroom is the school stage ; they will even imagine the traverse curtain. The method is something like this. We are dramatizing, say, " Sir Patrick Spens." The boy who is acting as " chorus" commences to read, " The King sits in Dunfermline town."

The master, in an undertone, supplies the stage direction " Curtains open, 3." The class understand the traverse curtain to open, revealing the King, the " eldern knight," and other courtiers. On the second line—" Drinking the blude-red wine "—the King mimes the action of drinking. The King then speaks his own words (he knows they are his because of the " quote marks ") :

> " O whare will I get a skeely skipper
> To sail this new ship o' mine ? "

So it goes on till the King sends his letter to Sir Patrick Spens who " was walking on the strand." Here the master, in his stage manager's whisper, says, " Scene II. ' The Strand.' Front stage. Enter Sir Patrick, 5." This gives Sir Patrick his entrance, and lets the class assume that the traverse curtain is now closed, so that any movement of the King and the other characters who were in Scene I. is not considered as coming within their ken. The next scene will be announced on the back stage, with Scotland on one side and " Noroway " on the other.

If the classroom dramatization is planned on these lines it will be found to proceed quite smoothly, and, furthermore, at the end of term the master can leave the pupils to rehearse on their own, and to fill in the outline with their own details. Boys of eleven will need the master's help to solve the practical problems of stage management when properties are introduced ; boys of fourteen can be left almost alone.

Stage Properties.—Properties—at all stages—should be quite simple and quite frankly " of the theatre." An attempt at full-blooded realism will destroy the whole convention, upon the acceptance of which the effect of the presentation depends. It is much better that Lochinvar's steed should consist of a cardboard head on a broomstick than it would be to bring on a real horse ; indeed, the whole thing may well be mimed. The acceptance of the convention once secured, all things are possible. For example, in the opening scene of " Sir Patrick Spens " the traverse curtains are looped open to reveal the King seated on a laboratory stool at the top of some property steps. He has a cardboard crown, and his cloak is a coloured table-cloth ! On each side of him is a property banner ; behind, a short length of " battlement " against a blue sky-cloth. It makes a pleasing picture without trying to disguise the means employed. It prepares the audience to " accept " the voyage in the third scene.

The Gude Ship.—In the classroom the " gude ship " may consist of a row of five or six boys, close together, hands on shoulders. With a little practice they will learn to " dip " one after the other, so as to give the effect of the undulating motion of the vessel. On the stage the ship may be more ambitious. A plank about 8 feet long is carried by the " crew " at waist height ; from it hangs a curtain, hiding the legs of the mariners, and long enough to sweep the floor, irrespective of the plunging of the ship ; at the ends are prow and stern pieces of painted cardboard. Very amusing results can be obtained if a piece of blue fabric, 6 or 8 feet wide, is laid across the stage floor and oscillated from either end to produce " waves." This oscillation increases when, on the homeward voyage, the sea grows " gurly," and the back edge of the strip is gradually raised up as the waves come " o'er the broken ship "—by this time plunging furiously—the front edge remaining weighted on the stage floor. Finally, the vessel disappears from view, and the waves gradually subside. But now a vertical wall of " water " stands across the stage :

> " Half owre, half owre to Aberdour,
>   'Tis fifty fathom deep."

The two operators in the wings [1] then lift the " sea " a foot or two to clear the stage floor, revealing the wreck of the vessel :

> " And there lies gude Sir Patrick Spens
>   Wi' the Scots lords at his feet."

The scene can be made more thrilling by lighting and " effects." When the " lift " grows dark the electrician gets busy with the dimmers. When the wind blows loud the stage manager starts a record of " wind and sea."

---

[1] It does not in the least matter that the audience is aware of these operators ; they can stand boldly on stage if they wish. What does matter is that the actors— like Bottom and his friends before the Duke—should perform with grim seriousness.

It may be advisable to omit some of the verses (*e.g.* verses 16–22) to prevent the anticlimax of a too protracted death on the part of the vessel, and it is to be feared that the chorus may have some difficulty in making itself heard above the laughter in the auditorium !

While these ballads of sturdy action are usually amusing to watch in performance, others may be deeply beautiful and moving. *Ballads and Ballad Plays* (Nelson) contains some excellent examples of both types, together with interesting suggestions on performance. A really beautiful example of a ballad play (with something of the quality of *The Immortal Hour* about it) is *The Hidden People*, by H. Noel-Paton, which was first performed by a school in York. (Allen and Unwin. 1s. 6d.)

The " chorus " may be an individual, or a group of half a dozen or more. A group, of course, will need considerable rehearsal in the speaking of their lines. The chorus should stand at the side of the front stage as near to the proscenium as possible. (In the absence of a traverse curtain, however, it has been suggested that the chorus might stand in a row at the back of the stage, and that players could wait their turns behind it.) Lighting the chorus by spotlight will be found effective, for the spot may be dimmed or intensified as it is required to focus the interest of the audience.

Some ballads, such as " On the bonny coast of Barbary," lend themselves to a singing chorus in addition to the spoken one. Some ballads, too—" Lochinvar " is probably an example—are best done entirely in mime, the chorus speaking all the words. In such cases the chorus can consist of several persons, each one speaking a different part, and perhaps joining in unison for the narrative passages. It is sometimes recommended (*e.g.* in *Ballads and Ballad Plays*) that the mimers must move throughout to the strict rhythm of the verse. There are many occasions, however, when to insist on this is to limit unnecessarily the scope of the players—to .

hasten unduly Lochinvar's swimming of the Eske River, or to curtail the " racing and chasing on Cannobie Lee." On the other hand, experiments with verse rhythms are often interesting ; the writer once attempted a mimed version of Milne's " King's Breakfast," where every action and gesture fitted the rhythm of the spoken words, and where every pause was allotted a definite number of beats.

Incidental music can be employed upon occasion, either to suggest the mood of scenes or to fit the actions (*e.g.* the " galliard " in " Lochinvar "), but its appropriateness will depend upon how far it is desired to preserve the *verse* rhythm.

The method normally employed in classroom dramatizations of ballads of allotting the narrative parts to the chorus and the dialogue to the characters may be followed in the dramatizing of other works. The writer has found it most conspicuously successful with *The Wind in the Willows*—that perfect book !—with boys of eleven. It was their suggestion originally. We had been acting various ballads, and they suggested doing the same with the book. So we set to work arranging suitable scenes, and were surprised to find how much could be acted simply as it stood. It is one thing to make a full-blown play from it—a *Toad of Toad Hall* ; another and much simpler to act little scenes linked together by narrative.

For example, Chapter VI., which deals with the running away of Toad, can be divided into five or six scenes. Scene I. will be " Rat's Room. Breakfast-time." The Rat and Mole take their places at the table, and the master reads the introductory narrative. When the " heavy knock " sounds at the door the characters take up their parts for themselves, the master filling in occasional stage directions from the narrative, " skipping " judiciously. Scene II. will be in the Hall of Toad's House, Scene III. in Toad's Bedroom. Scene IV. will be the short but gloomy scene at lunch after Toad has escaped.

The scene where Toad steals the car could be acted, but is better just read. The next scene is in the Magistrate's Court, and after the master has read the account of Toad's journey to prison, his final committal can be performed at the side of the " stage."

3. Mime

Mime is where poetry and dance join hands, where the spirit and the body express themselves in harmony together.

As an instrument of education it is difficult to overestimate its value, for, as Irene Mawer points out, education is not merely accumulation of facts, nor the conforming of mind and body to certain formulæ, but " the gaining of spiritual and physical poise." She sees in mime " the key to much that has baffled educational experts in the uniting of physical education with mental development." It may, indeed, be said to link together that *physical awareness* of things (of which it has been D. H. Lawrence's chief service to his day and generation to have reminded us) and mental perception or experience. " If our minds are to be really beautiful, healthy, alert *and* expressive, and our spirits full of sympathy and human kindness, then our bodies must be so too." [1]

Acting is the art of expressing things by the human body— by voice and movement. It is clear that if it is based upon early training in mime (or eurythmics) it will gain correspondingly in bodily expressiveness. The practice of dramatic schools is based upon this fact. Komisarjevsky makes his pupils walk about the stage for hours, moving to music. And Stanislavsky describes how he tried to develop in his pupils " not the outward rhythm of movement and action, but the inner rhythm of that unseen energy which calls out movement and action "—" To the accompaniment of a pianist's im-

[1] Mawer.

provisations, the pupils lived for hours in rhythm, explaining in their actions how they felt the music . . ."

The development of this subject is beyond the scope of this book (and the power of the writer) ; it can be pursued, by those seriously interested, in the books of Irene Mawer and Jaques-Dalcroze, and in *Mimes and Miming*. (See page 197.) For an account of mime used in the course of jolly classroom games as a way of conveying meaning, without too much thought of grace, the well-known chapter in *The Play-Way* may be consulted.

If mimed items are performed upon a stage before an audience, all that has been said in earlier chapters about masking and grouping, lighting and costumes, applies. The illustration on Plate I. shows what beautiful postures and groupings are possible. With mime, as with acting, the amount of liberty which can be allowed to individuals will depend upon the number upon the stage at once. The hero may be left to do as he likes when he is alone, but if the same freedom is granted to his troops when they enter there will soon be chaos. With crowds on the stage, as in the State, more law may mean more liberty—more, not less, opportunity for individual expression.

Miming that makes very little technical demand upon the players may none the less be very effective theatrically. For instance, at a recent show we embarked upon a burlesque of the Chauve-Souris in the " Volga Boat Song." Figures were grouped straining at the rope, in silhouette against a blue-green sky—with just an amber spotlight touching here and there the bent shoulders—while the song was sung (in real Russian !) by a choir performing on the radio-gramophone. We had devised an anticlimax which I will not divulge lest it be brought to the ears of M. Balieff, who would feel himself ill-repaid for the little kindnesses he has shown the writer. But when we saw the scene at the lighting rehearsal we decided that the grouping should be presented as a serious pictorial accompaniment to the music. As for the setting, the formal silhouettes of two cypress trees—made of thin card nailed to a plank—concealed two wooden posts which could not be removed (those in Plate X.). A few steps, covered with sacking, enabled us to group the figures as if they were mounting an incline, and spotlights, placed on the floor near the proscenium, sent horizontal shafts of deep blue light across the front of the stage, through which this erection and the figures themselves were seen as through a dim atmospheric mist, so that amazing improvisations of costume were possible. The swaying was controlled by a kind of tug-o'-war coach operating in the wings. The whole thing took very few minutes to arrange, and was adjudged exceedingly effective.

4. Dance

Items under this heading may—or may not—proceed from the ordinary work of the school. In girls' schools it is to be expected that they will, and in boys' schools folk-dances, morris dances, or Scandinavian dances can be adjusted to afford agreeable stage spectacle. There are also other kinds of dance ! One or two of them may be hinted at.

The curtains open to disclose columns of black curtains hanging silhouetted on a dim stage against a blue-green sky. The music of the " Faery Song " from *The Immortal Hour* is heard. If the audience possess any imagination the scene forces them to use it. The music changes into that of Schubert's *Moment Musical* ; three dimly-lit figures (the smallest boys you can find), in elfish or Greek costumes, dance, as skilfully as may be, about the columns ; the lights fade, the music dies away ; curtain. Applause (you must hope) ; encore. The curtains open, the lights come up, brighter than before, and on trip—in brief yet classical draperies—the three stoutest fellows that the upper school can provide. They go through the same motions of the dance, footing it here and there, sometimes " featly," sometimes not. Here is the essence of burlesque. You touch the audience with beauty one moment, and have them laughing at themselves the next.

On one occasion some boys who had been trained in various dances in an opera attempted a transposition of their movements into the modern American idiom. Their efforts were so amusing that every year since then has seen a burlesque dancing troupe which, for precision and ingenuity of movement, seems (at the moment) to put Mr. Cochran's Young Ladies definitely into the second class. As has already been hinted, this is a great opportunity for young electricians to indulge their lust for coloured light, and even a " rag " number of this kind can be made, very simply, to possess a certain artistic validity.

The arrangement of a revue programme, it may be said, calls for very careful thought. It would not do, for instance, to follow an item like that just mentioned with a play like $X = O$. Intervals between items must be exceedingly brief (witness how M. Balieff does it !), and items which demand considerable scene-setting are best introduced at the beginning of each of the two or three sections into which the programme is divided.

5. A One-Act Play

This section contains some suggestions for the production of John Drinkwater's $X = O$.* This play is chosen both because it is intrinsically well worth attempting by schools, and because it illustrates the thesis underlying this book. Its successful presentation depends upon something far more than acting ; it springs to life in the theatre from the perfect fusion of the " contributory arts."

* In "Ten Modern Plays," edited by John Hampden. (Nelson, cloth gilt, 1s. 3d.)

The Story of the Play.—$X = O$ is a tale of Trojans and Greeks towards the end of the ten years' war. In their tent on the plain before Troy we see two young Greeks, Salvius and Pronax. The beauty of the night leads them to talk of home, of their dreams and poems and aspirations for a nobler State—all now set aside for the business of slaughter—until Pronax has to steal forth through the starlight for a solitary raid upon the Trojan Wall.

In the next scene, on Troy Wall, we listen to two other young men, equally full of the promise of life, equally sensitive to the exaltation of beauty and to the futility of killing, until one of them, too, has to set out to do the thing he hates. He climbs down over the parapet. His friend, Capys, draws in the rope and paces the wall, saying to himself some verses. And then, a hand on the parapet, a sudden rush, and Pronax has his dagger in the Trojan's breast.

In Scene III. this action has its ironic counterpart ; the Greek poet Salvius, in his tent, is stabbed by the Trojan idealist Ilus. After a while Pronax returns from his errand, and cleanses himself in the trough at the tent door, reflecting on the horror of his night's work.

Then he realizes that something is wrong, and looks into the tent to discover the truth—" There is judgment made." The scores are level. All is futility. $X = O$.

In Scene IV. no words are spoken. The body of Capys lies on the Trojan Wall in the starlight and silence. After a few moments the signal whistle for the rope to be lowered comes from Ilus below. There is a pause. The signal is repeated. There is a pause. The curtain slowly closes. The effect of this final scene, if it is properly handled, is overwhelming. It is superb " theatre."

" Beauty is broken."—Now from this outline two things about the production of the play will be at once apparent. First that there are four scenes in the short space of less than half an hour, and that long pauses between them, in which the tension is allowed to drop, will be fatal. The interval between Scenes III. and IV. in particular must be so short that the audience have no time to begin to talk.

Secondly, the main impression given by the settings must be the beauty of the starlit night. Pronax refers to it in the very opening words of the play :

> " So is the night often at home. I have seen
> White orchards brighten under a summer moon
> As now these tents under the stars "—

and almost the first words of Scene II. are when Ilus says :

> " They're beautiful, those tents, under the stars."

A little later his companion, Capys, says :

> " It is still upon the plain to-night, and the stars
> Are a lantern light against you . . .
> I am careful for you to-night in all this beauty
> Of glowing summer—disaster might choose this night
> So brutally, and so disaster likes."

It is the beauty of the night which links all the scenes together ; it is the element of universality in the play. And those last lines of Capys above have an almost symbolic significance. The whole theme of the play is the futility of the mutilation of beauty brought inevitably by war. " We know," says Salvius,

> " Even upon the flood of adoration
> That beauty passes. That's the tragic tale
> That is our world."

Ilus reflects grimly on the odd skill which has led him to kill a hundred Greek boys—" spoiled in their beauty by me whose desire is beauty ! "—and Pronax, returning to find his friend

dead, turns to look out into the night with a sudden bitterness
—" Beauty is broken.'' Those words might be the text of
the play.

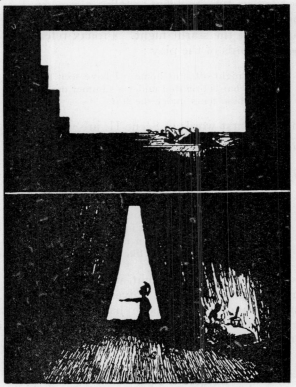

FIG. 42.—X = O : (a) Scene 4 ; (b) Scene 1.

The Setting.—The practical problem, then, is to express
this idea in settings that can be rapidly changed. The illustrations show one method of solving it. At the back of the
stage hangs a plain sky-cloth. (A in the plan, Fig. 43.)   A

yard or so in front of it runs a terrace (B) raised about 2 feet
from the stage. It is better if this is substantial enough to
bear weight without any creaking, though its chief purpose
is to screen the lights at the foot of the back-cloth. At one
side a few small rectangular flats (C) are arranged to suggest
vaguely a buttressed erection ; they will be seen only in
silhouette so that they need no special painting, but care
must be taken that they are opaque. For the innermost one,
beside which Pronax appears to climb up, we used a small
wooden box (D). (This climbing up and down must be well

Fig. 43.

rehearsed if the audience are to believe that there is a big drop
over the wall ; even if Pronax's body is in part behind the box
or flats, his head when it appears must move vertically upwards ; and he must avoid stepping between the ground-lights
and the back-cloth, or his shadow will be seen.) Farther along
the wall some steps or blocks (E) may give an added sense of
form.

All this stays permanently throughout the action. For
the tent scenes the traverse curtain (F) is pulled nearly across,
and to break the hard line some sacking or other material is
thrown over such part of the wall or steps as can be seen
through the tent door. The ground-lights (G) at the foot of

the back-cloth are dimmed down, and in the blue mist from the overheads the sacking can well be mistaken for landscape !

Properties needed for the tent scenes are (1) a couch for Salvius (H) ; (2) a lighted torch (I) ; (3) a trough (J) ; and perhaps (4) a stool or couch from which Pronax can take up his cloak and armour (K). For (1) we used the top sections of the gym " horse " covered with a curtain ; for (2) a bicycle lamp burner with the wick fed from a phial of oil held in a cardboard roll which was stood in a property vase *screwed* to a wooden stool to prevent any overturning ; and for (3) an ordinary camp canvas wash-basin.

For changing scenes these props can be moved into the wings, or into the dark front corners of the stage, in a few seconds if every member of the stage crew is allotted a specific job. This must be done very quietly, for the audience will be in darkness.

An actual scene-shifting plot is appended below.[1]

The stage manager's property plot will also include the cloak and armour which Pronax has to don, the water-jug borne by the servant, a cloth for Pronax to dry his hands after washing, and he will see that the actors have their hand props ready—Salvius his poems, Ilus his dagger, and so on.

The Lighting.—The lighting is all-important. The back-cloth is flooded with the deepest blue available, with perhaps a

---

[1] SCENE-CHANGING PLOT

(This is pinned up prominently, and in addition each boy is given his instructions written.)

After Scene I. and Scene III.   Front curtains, Hunter.
Extinguish light and remove lamp-stool, England.
Open traverse, Jones and Smith (we hadn't bothered to rope it for single-pull opening).
Remove trough, Johnson.
Remove couch, Mr. W. and Mr. B.
Remove sacking, Jones.
Remove stool for cloak, Smith.
After Scene II.   Replace props in same order.

little purple, all dimmed as low as necessary. There is no need to attempt actual stars—which could be done by bulbs behind the back-cloth. They may make the audience say " Ooh-er," but the diffused light from the plain cloth will better suggest the velvet quality of the starlit night. Some of our audience thought that there were actually stars in our sky ! In the tent scenes a little very dim amber overhead may be used in front (though it is not essential), and an amber spot or acting-area flood over the couch to suggest the spread of light from the torch. Another spot, quite dim, can be used to catch the expression on Pronax's face as he turns from the entrance. (It must be kept off the curtains, for the audience must not be conscious of it.) There will, of course, be no footlights. In the first scene on the wall the two men can be picked out faintly with spots, if necessary—but from the sides or overhead, not from the front, as shadows on the back-cloth would be fatal.

For the final tableau (Fig. 42 *a*) a faint spot may catch the outlines of the figure. At one of our performances we tried a rather daring experiment that it may be interesting to describe. Our intention was to suggest that the dead soldier on the walls of Troy was the dead soldier of all time. The light on the back-cloth was gradually dimmed right out, so that the figure lay in blackness, picked out by a spot which had something of green in it. And then the sound of modern machine-gun fire and artillery was heard—amplified through valves and a loud speaker from records. After a while it died away and the curtain *slowly* closed. I hope Mr. Drinkwater would have approved.

The Action.—The action itself requires little comment. Avoid restlessness when the pairs of soldiers are talking together. Pronax will be standing at the tent door when the curtain rises, and he can stay there silhouetted, perhaps with one hand clasping the droop of curtain, until he has to stir

himself for his expedition. The mood of both Scenes I. and
II. must be one of meditation till action cuts across. Pronax
must steer clear of hysteria in his final passage—even that
must be in a quiet key. The speaking, of course, must attempt
to do justice to the beauty of the words, and particular emphasis should be given—by a slight anticipatory pause, a
change of inflexion or of pitch, or a retardation of speed—to
the passages which carry a significance of tragic irony.

For example, the query of the Greek :

> " And Salvius,
> What of your songs ? "

has its parallel in the question of the Trojan, " What of your
sea-girl ? " and both responses point the lesson of the waste
of war. The generous sympathy of Salvius—

> " And those who weep, I think, are as those would weep
> If I should fall "—

has its counterpart in the feeling of Ilus how well might those
he killed and he

> " have thriven
> Together, conspiring this or that of good
> For all men."

(And is there a deliberate echo in the words, " If I should
fall," to remind us of another poet akin in spirit to these two ?)
So, too, the two idealists echo each other's thoughts, intensify-
ing the impression of the waste of potential good :

> " I was to build
> A cleaner state ; I dreamed a policy
> Purer than states have known."

So dreamed Pronax, while Ilus says :

> " It would be grand
> If Troy would use us as we might be used,
> To build and sing, and make her market-places
> Honest " . . .

BIBLIOGRAPHY

† Specially recommended.

Handbooks on Production

THESE, once rare, are now numerous. The best and most comprehensive are Milton Smith's *Book of Play Production* † (Appleton. 1926. 12s. 6d.), written for schools and colleges in the States, where play-production is a more serious business than it has hitherto been with us; C. B. Purdom's *Producing Plays* (Dent. 1930. 7s. 6d.), written for amateurs; and Jeffreys and Stopford's *Play Production* † (Methuen. 1933. 7s. 6d.), for amateurs and schools. Monica Ewer's *Play Production for Every One* (Noel Douglas. 1924. Out of print; 1929. 4s.); Parson's *Amateur Stage Management* (Pitman. 2nd Edition, 1931. 7s. 6d.); Sladen-Smith's *Amateur Producer's Handbook* (University Press, London. 1933. 2s.); Edward Lewis's *The Producer and the Players* (Allen and Unwin. 1933. 2s. 6d.); and Susan Richmond's *Textbook of Stagecraft* (Year Book Press. 1932. 3s. 6d.), concerned mainly with acting,* are likely to be found useful in, roughly, that order. There are deliberate omissions from this list. Rodney Bennett's delightful *Let's Do a Play !* (Nelson. 1933. 3s. 6d.) contains chapters on production, stage-management, scenery, lighting, etc., for amateurs with limited funds and equipment, is fully illustrated, and concludes with 140 pages of plays and recitations.

Scene Design

The best introductions to modern theory and practice are

* As is *The Technique of Play Production*, by A. K. Boyd (Harrap. 1934. 5s.), a man with experience of school work.

Sheldon Cheney's *Stage Decoration* † (Chapman and Hall. 1928. Out of print. 256 illustrations), and Fuerst and Hume's *Twentieth Century Stage Decoration* (Knopf. 1929. Approx. £9. Vol. I., text ; Vol. II., plates). There are also beautiful illustrations in Léon Moussinac's *The New Movement in the Theatre* (Batsford. 1931. £10, 10s.). Note especially Jesner's settings for *Richard III.* and *Othello* (Plates 39, 40) ; the dramatic lighting of crowds in Plates 51, 52, 111, 112, 113, 126 ; the use of levels in *Phèdre* (Plates 83, 84) ; the use of screens in *Twelfth Night* (Plates 75, 76). The special value of this book is that several illustrations are given of each production. Accounts of many of these productions will be found in Macgowan and Jones's *Continental Stagecraft* (Benn. 1923. Out of print), which is itself illustrated by a leading scene designer. The article on " Stage Design " † in *Encyclopædia Britannica*, 14th Edition, Vol. XXI., contains plates illustrating screens, unit, and abstract settings.

For designs, as distinct from records of productions, see those published in the various works of Gordon Craig : *Towards a New Theatre* (Dent. 1913. £1, 6s.), challenging illustration, interspersed with pungent, if often tiresome, comment ; *Scene* (O.U.P. 1923. £2, 2s.), with a typically vague description of his " screen system " ; *A Production* (Oxford. 1930. £8, 18s. 6d.), and the others below.

Design in the Theatre (Studio. 1927. Out of print) is concerned mainly with the painter-designer, but should be seen. Lee Simonson's *The Stage is Set* † (Harcourt, Brace. 1932. 25s.), by the leading designer of the New York Theatre Guild, is one of the most interesting recent books on the theatre, full of robust common sense ; often profound and witty. Simonson has no patience with Craig. *Settings and Costumes of the Modern Stage*, by Komisarjevsky and Lee Simonson (Studio. Winter Number, 1933. 7s. 6d. and 10s. 6d.), is an admirable collection, arranged by countries.

Textbooks on Scenery and Staging

Selden and Sellman, *Stage Scenery and Lighting* † (Harrap. 1931. 12s. 6d.). Invaluable. (See page 97.)

R. A. Wilson, *The Small Stage and its Equipment* (Allen and Unwin. 1930. 5s.). *Scenic Equipment for the Small Stage* (Allen and Unwin. 1933. 2s. 6d.).

Krows, *Equipment for Stage Production* (Appleton. 1928. 5s.).

Milton Smith (see above) has useful sections.

Scene-Painting

Van Dyke Browne's *Secrets of Scene-Painting* (Routledge. 1913. 5s.) is concerned with perspective methods ; so is F. Garnett in the chapters on " Painting," in *Simple Art Crafts and Stage Crafts for Schools* (Methuen. 1926. 3s.). For the book of Polunin (Beaumont. 1927) see page 100.

The best material is in Selden and Sellman.

Lighting

The books of Harold Ridge, of the Cambridge Festival Theatre, *Stage Lighting* † (Heffer. 1928. 5s.), *Stage Lighting for Little Theatres* (1925. Out of print), are invaluable.* Sellman is excellent, but his terminology is American. For the theory of colour see the standard work of M. Luckiesh, *Colour and its Applications* (Constable (U. S. A.). 1915. About 24s.), especially Chapters III. and XII., or the same writer's *Lighting Art : its Practice and Possibilities* (McGraw Hill Publishing Company. 1917. Out of print).

* See, too, his admirable articles in *Theatre and Stage*.

Costume

For historic reference the standard works are those of Ashdown (*British Costume during Nineteen Centuries.* Jack. 1910. 21s.), Calthrop (*English Costume.* Black. 1907. 12s. 6d.), Planché (*History of British Costume.* Bell. 1900. Out of print), Kelly and Schwabe (*Historic Costume : A Chronicle of Fashion in Western Europe,* 1490–1790. Batsford. 1930. 25s.), and Köhler (*History of Costume.*† Harrap. 1929. 25s.). For specific periods, Lester's *Historic Costume* (Batsford. 1925. 12s. 6d.) contains chapters on Greece and Rome, and Stone's *Bankside Costume Book* † (Wells Gardner, Darton. 1929. 3s. 6d.) is the best thing on the Elizabethan period, and is most practical. Hughes' *Dress Design* † (Pitman. 1926. 12s. 6d.) contains patterns. *A Book of Dramatic Costume,*† by Dabny and Wise (Harrap. 1930. 10s. 6d.), deals with all periods, and has excellent advice on the colour problem. Komisarjevsky's *The Costume of the Theatre* is an amusing historic survey of theatre practice (Geoffrey Bles. 1931. 25s.).

Make-up

So far as this can be learnt from books, see Eric Ward's *Book of Make-up* (French. 1930. 3s. 6d.), Parson's *Guide to Theatrical Make-up* (Pitman. 1933. 5s.), Chalmers's *Art of Make-up* (Appleton. 1925. New Edition, illustrated, 1930. 6s.), and the second part of Redgrove and Foan's *Paint, Powder, and Patches* (Heinemann. 1930. 7s. 6d.). The chapter in Jeffreys and Stopford is excellent.

Shakespeare

The most useful books for the producer are Granville-Barker's *Prefaces to Shakespeare* † (Two Series, Sidgwick and Jackson. 9s. each), indicating methods of approach ; and Roy Mitchell's *Shakespeare for Community Players* (Dent. 1919. 6s.),† which has good sections on properties and dresses, and sound advice on grouping and on playing in an arras setting. For the physical conditions of the Elizabethan playhouse the various studies of W. J. Lawrence, *The Elizabethan Playhouse* (Two Series, Shakespeare Head Press. 1913. 12s. 6d. each), *The Physical Conditions of the Elizabethan Public Playhouse* (O.U.P. 1927. 7s. 6d.), *Pre-Restoration Stage Studies* (O.U.P. 1927. 23s.), also *Shakespeare's Workshop* (Blackwell. 1928. 5s.), and L. B. Campbell's *Scenes and Machines on the English Stage* (Cambridge. 1923. 15s.), should be consulted.

On the Acting of Shakespeare's Plays, by C. M. de Reyes (Blackie. 1928. 2s. 6d.), contains detailed suggestions ; a well-meant attempt to do the producer's thinking for him.

Drama and Education

For the dramatic method in the classroom, see Caldwell Cook's *Play-way* (Heinemann. 1917. 8s. 6d.), and Chapters X. and XIV. of Mackaness's *Inspirational Teaching* (Dent. 1928. 10s. 6d.). There are interesting essays on the subject prefaced to *Perse Play Books*, Nos. 1 and 3. See also Finlay Johnson's *The Dramatic Method* (Nisbet. 1911. 3s. 6d.) ; Irene Mawer's *The Art of Mime*—especially Part III. (Methuen. 1932. 7s. 6d.) ; Jaques-Dalcroze's *Eurhythmics, Art, and Education* (Chatto. 1930. 8s. 6d.) ; *Drama in Adult Education* (H.M.S.O. 1s.).

Speech Training

H. C. Wyld's *The Teaching of Reading* (Murray. 1924. 3s.). Elsie Fogerty's *Speech Craft* (Dent. 1930. 3s. 6d.). Marjorie Gullan's *Speech Training in the Schools* (Evans. 1929. 1s. 6d.), *Spoken Poetry in the Schools* (Methuen. 1926. 3s. 6d.), and *Choral Speaking* (Methuen. 1931. 3s. 6d.). Kathleen Rich's *The Art of Speech* (Methuen. 1932. 3s. 6d.). A. M. Henderson's *The Art of Effective Speech* (University of London. 1931. 2s. 6d.). K. Emil-Behnke's *Speech and Movement on the Stage* (O.U.P. 1930. 7s. 6d.).

Lists of Plays

A List of Plays for Girls and Women. A List of Plays for Boys and Men. Compiled by the Junior Drama Committee of the British Drama League. Each gives over 200 plays, classified and fully annotated (Nelson. 1934. *Each* 1s.).

A List of Plays for Young Players. Fully annotated list of 370 plays (Nelson. Revised edition in preparation.) *One Thousand and One Plays for Little Theatres,* edited by Frank Shay (Appleton. 1923. 5s.). *Plays for High Schools and Colleges,* published by the National Council of Teachers of English, 506 West 69th Street, Chicago.

Model Stages

H. W. Whanslaw, *Everybody's Theatre.* Describes how to make a puppet theatre (Wells Gardner, Darton. 5s.).

A. Smith, *The Scenewright: the Making of Stage Models and Settings* (Macmillan. 1926. 10s.). Contains several very helpful chapters on the construction of models of sets.

A. E. Wilson, *Penny-Plain, Twopence Coloured* (Harrap. 1932. 21s.). A delightful history of the old juvenile toy-theatre drama, amusingly illustrated.

General

Gordon Craig, *On the Art of the Theatre* † (Heinemann. 1911. 10s. 6d.), *The Theatre Advancing* (Constable. 1924. Out of print). Containing some of the most stimulating and provocative essays on the theatre ever written.

C. Coquelin (Translator, Elsie Fogerty), *The Art of the Actor* † (Allen and Unwin. 1932. 3s.). A little classic.

Stanislavsky (Translator, J. Robbins), *My Life in Art* † (Geoffrey Bles. 1925. 30s.).

Allardyce Nicoll, *British Drama* (Harrap. 1925. 3rd Edition, 1932. 10s. 6d.) : the best comprehensive historic survey, with valuable lists of plays. *Theory of Drama* (Harrap. 1931. 8s. 6d.) : the revised form of his *Introduction to Dramatic Theory*. *The Development of the Theatre* (Harrap. 1927. 42s.) : for methods of presentation and setting.

J. W. Marriott, *Modern Drama* (Nelson. 1934. 5s.). An illuminating survey of drama in England, Europe, and America from the time of Robertson and Ibsen to 1934, with reading lists and suggestions for discussion. Fully indexed.

Stuart Page, *The Law of the Amateur Stage* (Pitman. 1929. 5s.). A most valuable exposition of the law relating to licensing, entertainments tax, etc.

M. Steen, *Peepshow* (Nicholson and Watson. 1933. 4s. 6d.). An adventure in drawing-room and village dramatics for the junior school library.

T. H. V. Motter, *The School Drama in England* (Longmans, Green. 1929. 15s.). A historical survey of achievements in the chief public schools, which shows that school drama has been at its best when it has been original and creative, not imitative.

Edited by Harold Downs : *Theatre and Stage* (Pitman. 1934. 2 vols. 42s.). A very comprehensive work which appeared in fortnightly parts.

K. Capek, *How a Play is Produced* (Geoffrey Bles. 1928. Out of print). Whenever dispirited, let the producer read this. One of the funniest books ever written.

For Special Needs and Occasions

Play Production in the Club (National Association of Boys' Clubs. 6d.).

E. Stuart Monro, *Play Acting for Scouts and Others* (Brown and Ferguson. 2s. 6d.).

E. Martin Browne, *The Production of Religious Plays* (Allan. 1932. 2s. 6d.).

Isabel Chisman and Gladys Wiles, *Mimes and Miming* (Nelson. 1934. 2s. 6d.). A handbook which explains *exactly* what to do, and includes fourteen varied mimes without acting fees. Stage plans, etc.

Periodicals

Drama. Published by British Drama League, 8 Adelphi Terrace, London, W.C.2. 6d. monthly.

Theatre Arts Monthly. New York. The leading record of scene design, beautifully illustrated. 3s. 6d.

APPENDIX I

THE PLAY IN THE SCHOOL

Dramatic Society Organization

BY JOHN HAMPDEN, M.A.

SCHOOL dramatic work in Utopia is so delightful that one is often tempted to write about it. But Utopia is inhabited by Utopians, and this gives it such incalculable advantages that we in England, with all our imperfections on our head, are apt to be discouraged by the comparison—or irritated. So this article, which is required to be severely practical, will give merely a plain account of what was done in a Surrey Grammar School during a period of seven years, in the hope that the imperfections of the scheme may incite other schools to improve upon it.

The Dramatic Society's work concentrated upon the dramatic " occasions " in the school year, which were four :

1. *Speech-Day Play*, in September. Several times this enabled the society to do its best work. The choice was usually a modern one-act play, ranging from " The Poetasters of Ispahan " and " The Rehearsal " (Baring) to " Campbell of Kilmohr."

2. *Christmas Plays*, at the end of the winter term. An afternoon performance given free to the school, and two evening performances to the public. (Reserved seats, 1s. ; others, 6d.) The " bill " consisted of three short plays, sometimes abridgments, but usually modern one-act plays, chosen for contrast—

e.g. farce, tragedy, and morality. Two of these plays were produced by senior boys ; for the third the producer was responsible. This Christmas programme proved to be of great value. It gave not only an excellent opportunity to the boy-producers, but a chance for younger actors to show what they could do, and for the society to experiment in lighting, staging, and in types of play which it might hesitate to attempt in three-act form, such as fantasy and poetic tragedy. The chief successes were " The Beau of Bath," " Michael," " Allison's Lad," " Thirty Minutes in a Street," " Colombine," " Tom Thumb the Great," and " A Man of Ideas." The Christmas plays were a preliminary trial and training ground for the next " occasion."

3. *The " Big Play,"* given in the first week of March. An afternoon performance for the school (admission 1s.), and three evening performances for the public (reserved seats, 2s. ; others 1s.). This was the chief dramatic event of the year, and the most strenuous, for like the Christmas plays it was given in a hired hall, with a very inconvenient stage, so that scenery and lighting apparatus had to be installed under difficulties at hectic speed. The chief successes were " Captain Brassbound's Conversion," " Henry IV., Part I.," " She Stoops to Conquer," " The Cardinal," " Pygmalion," and " Macbeth." " Ancient and modern " plays were chosen alternately.

4. *Junior School Prize-giving Play,* in July. This was performed by IIIa. boys, the producer being responsible. A modern one-act play was always chosen, the most successful being " Catherine Parr " (Baring), and " The Princess and the Woodcutter " (Milne). This play, which was rehearsed in form, was the culmination of the year's oral work in English, and an opportunity for discovering actors of promise. It was a defect in the society's work, not overcome, that these young actors could rarely be given parts again for two or three years ; but the form-room acting of Shakespeare and of modern one-act plays gave them some opportunities, and the producer,

who was the English master, did his best to encourage acting talent.

The idea behind all the society's work is that the boy, who is to be treated as an individual person, is of more importance than the play (or the audience), but that the highest individual development is reached through team-work, and that corporate creation of a work of dramatic art is of great educational value. An actor was sometimes given a better part than he merited, nearly always with good results. There were a number of cases of members benefiting very noticeably in mind and character from the society's work, and there was no trouble with self-conceit or jealousy. Responsibility was progressively delegated to boys, so that the electrician and stage-manager became important people, and several holders of these offices distinguished themselves. During performances the stage-manager assumed full control of the stage, and the producer was gratified to find himself rather in the way on several occasions. Lighting equipment included an elaborate switchboard, three liquid dimmers, and battens and floodlights fitted with slides for gelatines. These were all made—and well made—by the electricians and their allies at surprisingly low cost, the work being based, with modifications, on Mr. Harold Ridge's invaluable books. The acquisition of a grey gauze sky-cloth, which is a good substitute for a cyclorama, stimulated lighting experiments, not the least valuable part of which was that they gave scientifically-minded boys an interest in obtaining artistic results. Stage-settings and properties were designed by the producer and made from his rough drawings or verbal instructions, with slight supervision. The best and most intelligent work was often done by the " duffers " of the classrooms, and there was much more enthusiasm for this than for the ordinary school manual work, because it was purposeful. Much of this work and all the rehearsing, except for the Junior School play, were done out of school hours. Rehearsals usually took about ten days for the Speech-day play, four weeks for the Christmas plays, and six weeks for the " Big Play." Rehearsal hours were thirty—sixty minutes a day, and two or three hours on Saturday morning. There was no interference with school work except during the week of the " Big Play."

The society acquired a constitution by accumulation of precedents. The executive committee consisted of the producer as chairman ; a secretary, whose duties were nominal ; a junior treasurer, who kept the accounts and the box-office —a good deal of work ; and two other members. The stage-manager was co-opted when he had won his spurs. This committee, which usually comprised the leading actors, dealt with all questions, including choice of play (from a considerable number submitted by the producer) and casting. It was usual to choose the plays which could be cast most satisfactorily, always with an eye to variety and a preference for large casts. (On several occasions every form in the upper and middle school was represented in the cast.) That the casting was done by the leading actors rarely caused any difficulty, and though the producer sometimes found himself unhappily in a minority of one, he never had to exercise a right of veto. The committee was elected annually by the society, which included every actor who had taken part in any production, and those craftsmen—elected by the committee—who had rendered good service.

The producer was responsible for all business management, except seating arrangements and sale of tickets ; another member of the staff supervised these, and the actual work was done by the junior treasurer. Advertisement was by a few small bills of unusual design, and chiefly by small printed announcements of the play, which the boys distributed to their parents, and to every one in the neighbourhood who was interested. A regular audience was secured, and receipts rose from £19 in the first year to £91 in the seventh. As a result the society was always self-supporting and unsubsidized from the first, although there was no membership subscription and no expenses whatever were incurred by the members—a point of some importance because the actors included a number of scholars from poor homes. There was, of course, no deliberate money-making, but every year the profits made possible the purchase of new equipment, and this sense of continuous progress contributed to the members' *esprit de corps* : they seemed always to combine hard work with loyalty, enthusiasm, and high-spirited enjoyment of every production.

From *Drama*—May 1929, Vol. vii., No. 8. Reprinted by permission of the Editor.

APPENDIX II

SHOULD THE ACTOR FEEL? THE "DIDEROT ANTITHESIS" AND THE SCHOOLBOY

"In order to call forth the emotion, we ourselves must not feel it."
COQUELIN.

"Those who'd make others feel must feel themselves."—BYRON.

THE quotations fairly epitomize the two sides of the age-old theatrical controversy. Should the actor "live" the part he plays while he is on the stage? There is unlikely ever to be complete agreement; some of the greatest actors and actresses declare that they are themselves profoundly moved by their parts as they act them, while others, equally great, are able to keep an audience on the verge of tears while they converse, *sotto voce*, with their stage partners on the afternoon's cricket and racing results.

The subject is discussed in many works on acting, but nowhere better than in the edition of Coquelin's *The Art of the Actor* recently brought out by Miss Elsie Fogerty. Coquelin insists that the existence of the actor is dual. "One part of him is the performer, the instrumentalist; another, the instrument to be played on. 'Number One' conceives the character to be created . . .; this model 'Number Two' realizes in his own person. . . . 'Number One' must be master of 'Number Two.' He who sees must govern. . . . In other words, the actor must remain himself even in those moments where the public, carried away by his acting, thinks him most

203

absolutely distracted. . . . Briefly, he must not experience a shadow of the sentiments he is expressing—at that very moment when he is expressing them with the greatest truthfulness and power. Study your part, enter into the skin of your character, but never abdicate : hold the reins. It is false, it is ridiculous to think that the height of the actor's art is to forget that he is before the public. If you no longer know where you are, you have ceased to be an actor ; you are a lunatic."

On the other hand one may quote Zamiatin who, describing the Moscow Art Theatre, says that " when Michael Chekhov acts Vershinin in Anton Chekhov's *Three Sisters,* he continues to behave like Vershinin even in the intervals. And it is not put on by any means ! In private life he is a phlegmatic and almost gloomy person. Yet I remember seeing him in his dressing-room between two acts of Gogol's *Revisor* . . . and even in the intervals Michael Chekhov continues to behave in the highly eccentric and undignified manner of Gogol's hero. It is almost uncanny to watch him. Kachalov, acting Ivan in *The Brothers Karamazov,* is magnificent—not, however, as a star turn, but because his impersonation or, shall I say, transfiguration is so complete. Stanislavsky has preached Yogism to his actors ; they must renounce the world ; they must meditate ; they must forget their own selves, and live themselves into their parts." *

But the antithesis is not so absolute as it may seem. Stanislavsky himself, who wrote that " nine-tenths of the labour of an actor lies in beginning to live and feel the rôle spiritually," and who went so far as to have himself shut up in a rat-infested dungeon that he might find inspiration for a part (an experiment that was *not* successful), wrote that " stage emotion is only one kind of hysteria," and that he found that in moments of strong upheaval, which he " mistook

* *The Manchester Guardian.*

for inspiration," it was not he who controlled his body, but his body that controlled him.

There is, at any rate, agreement that the actor must "feel" his part at some stage in his preparation of it, if not in his actual performance. Thus Coquelin says, "Have within you the spirit of your part, and you will naturally deduce all its externals . . . the soul creates the body, not the body the soul." And as for the emotion which certain actors experience during their performance, perhaps it can best be explained in the words of Miss Fogerty : "Certain actions, notably the technique of an art, like playing the violin or acting a tragic part, can become and remain subconscious, yet absolutely controlled by the 'watcher' in the brain. While on the other hand, the concurrent emotional delight in the perfect performance of an artistic masterpiece may inspire the musician or the actor with feelings almost as intense as the reality of experience."

What is the relevance of this discussion to acting in schools? Is one likely to find in boys that technical skill which can induce in an audience an emotion which the actor does not at the moment feel ? Occasionally, I have known boys who have moved an audience very deeply while simultaneously convulsing their colleagues in the wings with surreptitious words and by-play. Once indeed, when in a misguided moment I permitted myself to participate in a sketch, I had cause to suspect a determined and concerted (and, I regret to say, almost successful) effort on the part of my fellow-actors to make *me* laugh at the wrong time ! But so far as the presentation of serious drama is concerned, I have assumed that with the majority of juvenile actors technique will never be adequate to convey completely even the emotion which is genuinely there, let alone that which is not.

But recently, discussing the topic with a few members of the School Dramatic Society, I received a mild shock, and so I assembled all those boys who had at any time taken important parts in productions, and talked the problem over with them. I have seldom heard a more interesting discussion amongst boys than that which followed.

There was general agreement that a part had to be " felt " before it could be conveyed. Some said that they felt the emotion of their part when they first read it ; most agreed that it came to birth gradually during the course of rehearsals. Some said that they were still in the grip of their part when the play was being performed—that if they were called to " register " hate for another character they really felt it at the time ; that if they were required to look off-stage for an imaginary character, or at an imaginary landscape, they really saw the person or landscape in their mind's eye. But the majority (to my surprise) did not accept this view. Some few, indeed (and these included some who had been most successful in moving audiences by the charm and apparent sincerity of their acting), said that they felt nothing at all of what they were conveying ; that it was with them merely a matter of deceiving an audience.

The majority view was that the emotion was felt at the time of playing but not so intensely as to prevent the actor from being perfectly responsible for his words, business, and movement. As soon as the player ceased to be aware that he was acting, then he ceased to be acting. They thought that complete absorption was the most likely cause of " fluffing "— that an actor "living" the part in his own person might find himself wanting to go on in his own words. His sudden realization of what he was doing, and the attempt to come out of his dream state to reality, might cause his mind to " go blank " altogether.

I put the view to them that schoolboy acting-technique was not likely to be good enough to do what professional technique could do, and that an audience was more likely to be moved by sincerity of feeling which overflows, as it were, from the actor and communicates itself telepathically to the audience. Some of them questioned the validity of telepathy, so I instanced the common example of the indifferent orator who, eschewing tricks, " gets across " by sheer force of sincerity. They were good enough to concede that there might be something in the idea, always provided that the actor was not so carried away as to forget all that he had rehearsed. They agreed that if movements and gestures had been mechanized by constant rehearsal, they might form a subconscious basis for the player's performances—a skeleton, as it were, into which he could infuse life—but, they were insistent, he must keep his head.

One of them said that he found it a great help to " think himself into a character " just before making an entrance. If he knocked upon the door not in his own character but in his stage character, he felt himself more at home in his part when he was actually upon the stage. Some one recalled that in the dressing-room they habitually called one another by their playing names ; and they seemed disposed to agree that something of their stage personality persisted in the intervals.

While it would be unjustifiable to place too much reliance upon introspections of this kind, it is fairly obvious that boys differ as much on the stage as grown-up players. From an educational point of view, it is clearly better for the boy himself that he should feel his part sincerely than that he should learn how easy it is to fool an audience. Let him keep his head certainly, but let him put his heart into his part as much as he can. And if he be one who naturally stands aloof from his part, let him take care not to upset those who are more absorbed by theirs. For example, when conversation has to be " made " between people talking on the stage but unheard by the audience, let the talk be in keeping with the play ; let not some of the players indulge in remarks that may upset others, or throw them out of their parts.

Following our discussion, a number of boys felt sufficiently interested to set down their views (voluntarily !) in writing. I append extracts from three essays.

(The first essay is specially interesting, because the young writer had borrowed Coquelin's book from the Public Library and read it, and the views he expresses are the opposite of Coquelin's.)

1. The impression produced on an audience by an actor depends on a multitude of things, of which one of the most important is his success in creating an atmosphere of sincerity. In a school play the audience is largely composed of people who have come to see " Billy " or " Billy's friend Harry " act, and therefore one of the most necessary duties of the actor is to create the impression that he is neither " Billy " nor " Harry." If, at any time during the performance, one of the fond relations whispers " Billy is better than Harry," both actors have failed. The last thing the actor must do is to give the impression that he is a schoolboy dressed up ; he must seem to *be* his part, not merely to be imitating it. The atmosphere of realism may be obtained, say many excellent authorities, by good technique. But however good technique may be, it remains mere technique. It is a sham, and lacks sincerity. Those in the audience who have come merely to see their sons and friends may not notice this lack of sincerity, but it is for the people, however few, who love drama for its own sake that the School Dramatic Society works, and its members must try to aid those who want to forget their *sons'* presence on the stage.

Thus the schoolboy actor has a disability not experienced by the professional, as he has an audience unknowingly unsympathetic to the play, and having to act to his personal friends (whereas the professional is unknown personally to the bulk of his audience), he must, as it were, be doubly sincere.

Where technique alone will suffice for the professional, it will not do for the schoolboy.

Imagination is capable of all things, and if the boy goes on the stage firmly believing he *is* the part, his sincerity will communicate itself to the audience. If he is insincere, the audience may not consciously notice as much, but there will be something lacking in their own understanding of the play. . . . The actor must learn the words so that he speaks them without conscious effort of memory, and the dramatist must write such words as create a right atmosphere and do not impede the actor in imagining he is the part. Anachronisms and unnaturalness are the marks of a bad dramatist, which is one of the arguments for Earl Russell's assertion that Ibsen is a greater dramatist than Shakespeare ; Ibsen does not imagine Bohemian coasts or Roman striking-clocks. To act in a Roman play and hear clocks striking needs a terrific imagination—like that of the man who imagined himself to be a poached egg.

It cannot be asserted, of course, that the actor must not have his wits about him. In reality he must have two selves, the first of which lives the part, and the second of which controls the first. When a murder has to be committed, or a mistake in the playing rectified or smoothed over, " Number Two " must take " Number One " firmly in hand ; but when " Number Two " has too much power, sincerity and atmosphere suffer. (B. M. Hill. Age 16.)

2. From what little experience I have had on the stage, it appears to me that the actor does not " live " his part but he acts it.

Certainly, while saturated in the atmosphere of the play at rehearsal, the actor understands the emotions of the characters, and in a sense " lives " his part mentally for some short time. But this is just a temporary state of mind, useful to give the actor the appropriate gestures and tones ; it is not a permanent illusion, and it dies a natural death when its work is done. At subsequent rehearsals the actor can be in any state of mind he pleases ; for he has so memorized his actions and tones that he can reproduce them when desired, almost parrot-like. The highly emotional tension, which was once sincere, slackens, so that during the actual performance the actor's tone, manner, and gestures are only superficial, for now he has to play not to himself but to the gallery. Thus, the ghost in *Hamlet* may trip over the wiring and bark his shins on some unemployed " flat," but while cursing heartily under his breath, he is able simultaneously to thrill the hearts of the audience with his sepulchral tones.

If a schoolboy actor actually " lives " his part intensely, he will be inclined to speak his own words, take up his own positions, and assume his own actions, thereby disturbing the producer's plan, and consequent chaos will be unavoidable. No, the actor must remember that he *is* an actor, playing to an audience, angling for effect which mere sincerity cannot achieve, forced to exaggerate to " get it across," speaking slowly and deliberately, putting emphasis on words which hardly need it in ordinary life, indeed making all his words and actions seem unnatural and forced to himself, so that they may appear natural and effortless on the other side of the footlights. When he is speaking into the wings during an actual performance the actor no longer sees what the audience thinks he sees ; he has pictured the scene mentally during the primary rehearsals, and only the *effect* of the picture on his manner and speech remains ; the illusion has disappeared, but the impression is left, and the audience sees only the impression.

Acting, to me, is entirely superficial ; during the performance the actor should suppress his natural emotions, and what he says or does should be as unnatural and insincere as the lights and effects around him—and as impressive to the audience.   (H. Danskin. Age 16.)

3. Once the actor steps upon the stage his personality changes. He feels that he has to do something of which he alone is capable, and at the same time retain that sense of responsibility and level-headedness which is essential in every actor. A good actor should not need to be told his every action, but should feel prompted by some inner urging which tells him whether he is being awkward or otherwise. The man who feels awkward on the stage, and is scared to give vent to free and easy action, stamps himself as a bad actor; it is essential that ease and naturalness should be felt, and movement be unrestricted and unhampered. The actor should feel so at ease that nothing, however distracting, can take away his attention or upset his balance. There is, however, the danger of going to such an extreme that his surroundings are utterly disregarded, and he feels himself " carried away " by his part. This condition marks distinctively the bad actor. The moment he forgets the audience to which he is playing, forgets his surroundings, forgets himself in the depths of his part, at that moment he ceases to act. In reality he is deceiving both audience and self, for he is transforming himself forcibly into another person, and so far believes that he is that person that he goes on until the end of the play in a kind of trance. This is bad acting, for the simple reason that it isn't acting at all; the player should gain credit not for being a great actor but for possessing the ability to change his personality.

A good actor, on the other hand, should be fully conscious of all his actions upon the stage, and of their significance to the audience. He should be clear-thinking and exact, knowing where he should be upon the stage at any time and for what reason. He has these things in his head at the same time as he is " deceiving " the audience by his acting. He needs to be always a few speeches ahead of his audience. This shows that the actor himself, while on the stage, is really divided into two

people, and he is in himself both actor and audience. He
should be able to judge his own acting, and not require to be
told what is wrong. He should know instinctively, because
his " audience self " tells him. But a man cannot both
execute and judge his actions if he " lives " his part, for then
he will be really unconscious of that which he says and the
manner in which he is saying it. The good actor can alter his
voice and gestures at will ; the other remains a slave to his
own feeling.   (Norman Duncan.   Age 16.)

APPENDIX III

HOW TO MAKE A SWITCHBOARD

By Mr. H. Bambrough, M.Sc.

A STAGE switchboard differs from that of a factory or workshop in that the latter is usually a permanent structure, designed for a certain function, and this function remains unaltered from day to day or year to year. A stage switchboard, on the other hand, has to serve the fixed purpose of controlling and regulating all stage current, but this control and regulation differs not only from play to play, but according to the daily whims of the producer. It is essential, then, that the switchboard for stage purposes must be so designed that additional circuits may be added to it whilst it is " alive," and that circuits not in use may be disconnected, and this coupling or uncoupling must be done rapidly and simply by means of plugging or unplugging. It is never a job for an amateur electrician to connect circuits by means of screwdriver and pliers to a " live " switchboard, and all such dangerous connections must be eliminated. Again, in schools, the stage is usually of a temporary nature, erected for the period of the play, and consequently the switchboard has to be removed when the period of production is over.

The complete control of all circuits, so that intensities of illumination may be varied at different parts of the stage and just the exact tones and shades produced by the blending of different colours of varying intensities, is so necessary a part of successful play production that dimmers, either liquid or metallic, are essential ; it should be possible either to dim all circuits independently, which is the ideal, or, by coupling up circuits on one dimmer, to control just as many circuits as are required to produce a particular effect. Since dimmers of the metallic type are expensive, it rarely happens that any school can provide a dimmer for each circuit ; hence the necessity arises for building a switchboard of maximum flexibility, so that dimmers may be switched in to those circuits requiring them in a particular act, or the circuits may be switched on or off the dimmers. And all those additional lights which so add to the effectiveness of a setting—table lamps, standard lamps, acting area, and floodlights—all of a temporary nature, ought to be able to be plugged to the switchboard just as required. Nor is a switchboard of an elaborate or complicated type necessary to fulfil these requirements.

Most producers will find cost the dominating factor in the construction of a switchboard, but if a board is planned on a unit system from the first, it can be enlarged year by year as more money becomes available from the profits of successive productions. The system which I have designed is one which gives maximum flexibility, and can be used either for small or large boards by simply duplicating the unit.

The circuit diagram of the unit is given in Fig. 1. I have taken as the basis of this unit an ordinary four-way fuse-box such as is used for the distribution of lighting in houses. The size of the board initially should be large enough to accommodate the final requirements, and the first unit mounted well to the left-hand side to allow for any additions. The board itself should be of stout construction, but as slate is expensive, and drilling slate is not a task to be undertaken lightly, wood may be used providing it is thoroughly dry, and no bare wires are allowed to touch it. As an additional precaution, the face

of the board on which the components are mounted should be
covered with sheet tin, which should be connected to earth by
a stout lead soldered to it. This will prevent arc-ing across
the board and danger of shock due to leakage.

" A " in the diagram is the fuse-box; S_1, S_2, S_3, S_4, are
ordinary 5-amp. switches. (15-amp. switches are better, but

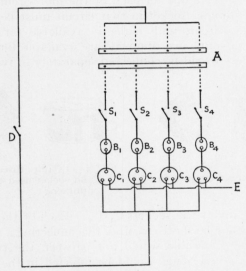

FIG. 1.—The circuit.

the 5-amp. will be large enough for circuits up to 1,000
or 1,200 watts.) These are mounted below the fuse-box.
Immediately below are the two-pin, 5-amp. sockets, B_1, B_2,
B_3, B_4, into which the stage circuits are plugged. (Fig. 2.)[1]
Directly below these two-pin sockets are the three-pin, 15-amp.
sockets, C_1, C_2, C_3, C_4, which are there for the purpose of plug-

[1] Switch and socket can be purchased built into one unit. This will save time
in wiring, but run up replacement costs.   E. F. D.

ging in the dimmers as required. (Fig. 3.) It should be noted that the third sockets in each of these are all connected by a common lead straight to earth.

The reason for three-pin sockets being used for the dimmers and two-pin sockets for stage circuits needs perhaps a little explanation. It may happen that there are not sufficient dimmers to provide one for each of the four circuits. Consequently the dimmer socket in that circuit must be shorted to complete the circuit and make it available for stage use. Assuming that only two dimmers are available for use in the first unit, these would be connected separately to two three-pin

Fig. 2. — 5-amp. two-pin plug and socket used to connect circuits to board.

Fig. 3.—15-amp. three-pin plug and socket used to plug in dimmers.

plugs fitting any of the sockets C_1–C_4. Each of the other two plugs would then be short-circuited by connecting a stout, well-insulated lead ($\frac{1}{18}$ cable would do) between the two pins of the plug, and these plugs would be inserted in the sockets of the circuits for which dimmers are not available. It is obvious that if the plugs for the sockets C_1–C_4 were of the same type as those for the lighting circuit sockets B_1–B_4, danger arises in the fact that a short-circuiting plug may be inserted in any of the sockets B_1–B_4, in which case the fuse in that circuit would be blown at once. With plugs and sockets of the types indicated no such danger can arise, since only the correct plugs can be fitted to the correct sockets.

D is a master switch, connected into the main circuit, so that all four circuits of the unit can be operated simultaneously without the use of the smaller switches S_1–S_4. It must be of larger carrying capacity than the circuit switches, since it has to pass the total current in all four circuits; hence if S_1–S_4 are 5-amp. capacity, D should be at least 15-amp. capacity. For switchboards in which more than 5 amps. are likely in each of the four circuits, D should be a quick break switch of the knife-edge type, and capable of carrying the total load of the unit.

The board, as indicated, is capable of taking four circuits, but this can be extended to twelve quite easily. To do this, four three-way adaptors (two-pin type) are obtained and plugged in to the sockets B_1–B_4. (Fig. 4.) The additional circuits are plugged in to the three-way adaptor, and thus twelve separate circuits can be accommodated. The disadvantage of this, of course, is that the three circuits plugged in to each of the sockets B_1–B_4 are grouped on one dimmer, and that dimmer will dim all of the three circuits together. It has, however, the advantage that where it is required to dim a number of circuits at the same time, these circuits can be plugged to one dimmer; and the fewer dimmers there are to operate together, the more efficient is the actual dimming likely to be.

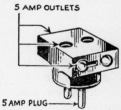

5 AMP OUTLETS

5 AMP PLUG

Fig. 4. — Three-way plug-adaptor for plugging in sockets to take three circuits.

The leads from the stage circuits *can* be of the ordinary house-lighting flex, which will carry 5 amps. without undue heating, provided it is heavy flex. But immediately funds are available, cab-tyre cable should be used. The two leads are brought through small holes drilled in the board, connected to a two-pin plug, and plugged in to one connection of the three-way plugs. Enough length of lead should be used to enable the circuit to be plugged in to any of the sockets B_1–B_4

(or B_1–B_8 or –B_{16}, if your unit is duplicated as described below). Similarly, the dimmers are connected by two leads through holes from the back of the board to three-pin plugs, and again these leads should be long enough to reach any of the sockets C_1–C_4 (or C_1–C_8, or C_1–C_{16}).

In wiring up the unit, it is of extreme importance that the cable used should be of such current-carrying capacity that it will safely take any current the board is likely to carry, otherwise the danger of fire arises through over-heating of the cable. Thus it is advisable for the constructor carefully to calculate what the maximum current through the board is likely to be. For the benefit of those without technical knowledge who may wish to construct a small board of this type, it might be advisable to stress a few fundamental principles which will assist in this calculation.

1. All circuits on the board are connected in parallel.

2. When electrical circuits are so connected, the total current (amperage) and the total consumption (wattage) are obtained by adding up the currents and the watts in the separate circuits.

3. Watts = volts × amps.

4. Amps. = $\dfrac{\text{volts}}{\text{ohms.}}$

Let us see how these simple facts may be applied in calculating the size of cable in the unit. Assume that when the board is carrying its maximum current, there are three circuits each of 1,000 watts at 250 volts plugged in to each T-piece in sockets B_1, B_2, B_3, B_4—twelve circuits in all. Since the circuits are all in parallel, the total wattage = 12,000. Hence the total current = $\dfrac{12,000}{250}$ = 48 amps. And current through each socket = $\dfrac{3,000}{250}$ = 12 amps. Hence under these conditions each fuse must carry 12 amps., and each socket and dimmer socket must be of the 15-amp. type, and the connecting leads must also carry 12 amps. safely.   The board could thus be wired with $\frac{3}{20}$ cable, with the exception of the lead through the master switch.   This lead takes all the current through the board, so it must be connected in with much heavier cable. A unit such as this is probably capable of supplying much more current to the stage than most schools will require, but the reserve is there should it be required, and further alterations are unnecessary.[1]

The advantages of such a unit are now fairly obvious. (1) Any number of circuits up to twelve can instantly be connected to the board by simply plugging in.   (2) For unified control, circuits can be grouped into one switch or one dimmer. (3) For rapid changes between acts, circuits may be plugged on to dimmers, or dimmers on to circuits.   (4) It is possible to plan beforehand just what connections to make or to alter to produce a given combination.   (5) The circuits may be switched out independently, or collectively by one master-switch if a complete black-out is required.

The aim underlying the design of the unit system was to overcome the lack of dimmers, which accounts chiefly for the grouping of three circuits on one dimmer.   Where more dimmers are available, the grouping of circuits is not so necessary; but to maintain the range and flexibility of the board and increase its capacity, all that is required is to build

[1] Actually, it would be disadvantageous to work with *all* your circuits of the wattage illustrated here, for not only would you need the 15-amp. sockets, etc., but your dimmers would have to be of 3,000 watt capacity, since 3 circuits of 1,000 watts might be plugged to each.   Unless your stage is very large, the only circuits of 1,000 watts you are likely to have are those for spots and floods ; if your battens are split up into colour circuits, as recommended in the text, each circuit will be of 500, 300, or perhaps only 250 watts.   You could therefore work on a basis of 1,000–1,200 watts per socket (for which 5-amp. sockets would suffice), and you could plug in to each either one 1,000 watt circuit (say, a spot), or three of 300, or one of 500 and two of 250.   But if your board is big enough to take all your circuits you will find it increases control if you have a number of small (preferably metallic) dimmers to take circuits of 500 or 750 watts, and also if you have upon your board at least one 15-amp. socket by means of which you can plug two or three 1,000 watt spot or flood circuits to one large (preferably liquid) dimmer.   E. F. D.

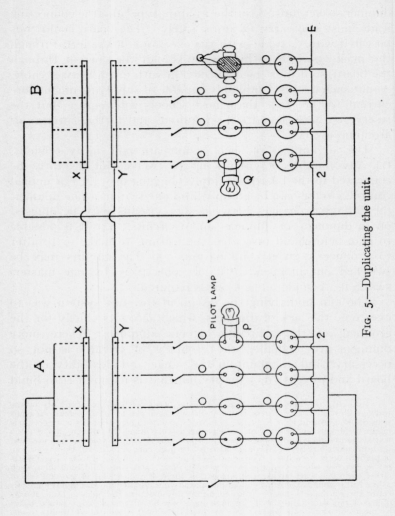

FIG. 5.—Duplicating the unit.

a second unit similar to the first, and connect both in parallel. Fig. 5 indicates how this is carried out. The only connections necessary between the two units are the two leads XX and YY between the bus-bars of the fuse-boxes, and to continue the common earth wire through the earth terminals of the dimmer plugs in the two units as at ZZ. The board now has double

FIG. 6.—(*a*) Secondary distribution board.

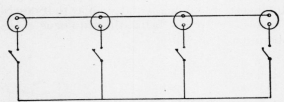

FIG. 6.—(*b*) Wiring circuit for secondary
distribution board.

the capacity so far as circuits are concerned, but the same flexibility is maintained with increased range and increased possibilities.

It sometimes happens that it is not possible to see the stage from the lighting platform, and where this is so, correct dimming becomes exceedingly difficult. To overcome this difficulty a pilot lamp may be inserted in parallel with each of the circuit sockets, which will be dimmed with the circuits plugged into that socket. The operator is thus able to watch his pilot lamps and judge the speed of his dimming from these. One pilot lamp only is shown in each unit in Diagram 5, at P and Q, any others being connected in similarly to the other sockets. Two leads are taken from the socket to a batten holder which is screwed to the front of the board, and the pilot lamps inserted in this.

Connecting the switchboard to the mains is not an operation I should recommend an amateur to attempt. Engage a competent electrical engineer to fix a mains switch and fuse of the quick make and break type and of the correct carrying capacity—e.g. 30 or 45 or 65 amps.—above where the switchboard will be fixed when in use. Then connect from the busbars of the first fuse-box to the two terminals of the mains switch. To ensure that any trouble due to blowing of fuses can be speedily rectified, keep a spare fuse-bridge ready wired, to replace at once a blown fuse.

The total cost of building a unit such as that described here is given below, the prices being the catalogue prices of the G.E.C. obtaining at present.

		s.	d.
1 four-way fuse-box		7	0
1 15-amp. S.P. switch		3	6
4 5-amp. bakalite S.P. switches . .		3	2
4 5-amp. two-pin sockets and plugs .		5	0
4 15-amp. three-pin sockets and plugs		14	2
4 three-way adaptors, 5 amp. . .		4	7
Cable for wiring		5	0
Wood		5	0
Total	£2	7	5

This, of course, does not include dimmers. Where slider dimmers can be purchased, they should be obtained and mounted on the base of the switchboard. Where, however, expense prohibits the buying of dimmers, quite efficient liquid dimmers may be made at very little cost. (See chapter on Lighting.)

It often happens that connecting the switchboard to side-floods, strip-lights, and other small lights at the far side or back of the stage means a lot of overhead leads, with consequent prodigal use of cable or flex. Much of this can be saved by adopting the device of subsidiary distribution boards, which can be constructed for a few shillings as follows: Mount on a wooden batten four or five batten-holders and wire them in parallel with $\frac{3}{20}$ cable. This will take any current likely to

FIG. 7. — Batten-holder and bayonet adaptor, as suggested for subsidiary distribution board.

be required. Now using cab-tyre cable, connect from one point on the switchboard to the first holder on the batten. The batten can usually be stowed away conveniently below the stage.[1] Any sidelights or additional small lights can now be wired to bayonet adaptors and plugged in as required. (Fig. 7.) The saving of cross-stage leads is obvious.

Finally, it is necessary to note that all portable lights, particularly floodlights and spotlights carrying large currents, should be earthed. To do this a third wire is connected to

[1] If this board is in such a position that live sockets may be a source of danger, safety may be ensured by fitting each socket with a switch, either separately mounted, or of the reading-lamp type. (Fig. 6.)   E. F. D.

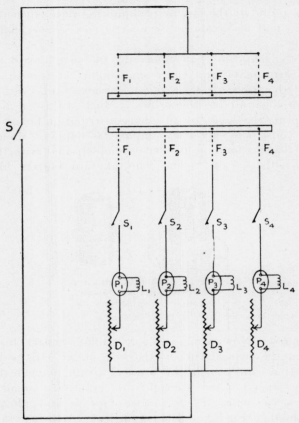

Fɪɢ. 8.—Complete circuit diagram of unit.

F₁–F₄, D.P. fuses (contained in fuse-box). S, master switch.
S₁–S₄, circuit switches. P₁–P₄, sockets (two-pin). D₁–D₄,
dimmers. L₁–L₄, pilot lamps.

the metal casing of the lamp and earthed. This can be done
by running the earth wire to the switchboard and connecting
to one of the earth pins on a three-pin plug. If the lamp is

far from the switchboard a shorter earth may be more convenient—but any good earth connection will do.

Fig. 8 is the complete circuit diagram of the unit, and Fig. 9 shows a school board made by repeating the unit four times.

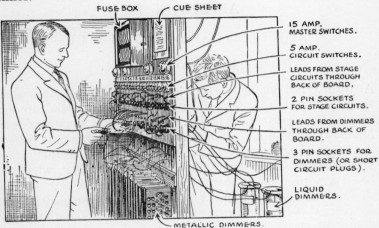

FIG. 9.—Sketch diagram of home-made switchboard able to accommodate 16 circuits of 1,200 watts, or 48 circuits of 400 watts. (Maximum load, 77 amps.)

APPENDIX IV

ADJUDICATING YOUNG PLAYERS

By John Hampden, M.A.

Adjudicating young players is not less difficult or less responsible work than adjudicating their elders—who are not always their betters. Though the best adult amateurs must obviously reach a much higher standard, and therefore present the adjudicator with much more advanced æsthetic and technical problems, young players of some ability, who have been ably and sympathetically produced for a few seasons, can do remarkably well. In freshness and imaginative sincerity, as well as in team-work, they can sometimes give points to their elders. And when both are at their worst there is little to choose between them.

The artistic problems, therefore, are usually much the same, and with junior players there are added complications. The best junior dramatic work is always educational, in the broadest sense of that somewhat unfortunate word, since it is certain to influence, and may influence profoundly, the development of the young player's personality. The first principle of such work should be that the player is more important than the play, and the play than the audience—a point of view very far removed from that of the professional theatre or the advanced amateur.

On the one hand, this makes it all the more important that the adjudicator should emphasize the need for the highest artistic standard possible in every detail of the production.

He knows that the producer may be sorely tempted to lower his artistic standard, from quite honourable motives—and he knows also that no audience gives such uncritical praise as an audience of parents.

On the other hand, the " educational " element must be kept clearly in mind. It is even more important to ask whether a company is moving in the right direction than to ask how far they have gone. The adjudicator should try to discover something of the conditions in which they are working, and then determine what allowances, if any, should be made. There are few more delicate tasks than judging a festival in which a company of players from a slum area appears with a company from cultured homes : the latter may begin (but not always !) at a point which the former can hardly hope to reach, and even if the difference is not allowed to affect marks it should be recognized by the adjudicator, with as much tact as he can muster, in his oral and written criticisms. A similar problem, perhaps even more troublesome, may be raised by two companies from the same institution which are obviously of different mental calibre.

Whatever the circumstances, however, it is of first importance that the criticism given should be constructive and encouraging, never the reverse ; that the adjudicator should try to show how a performance could be improved, not where it is wrong. Tone is important also. It is very easy to be clever at the expense of beginners ; usually it is cheap, and often it is fatal. Sarcasm must be avoided at all costs, and so must patronage—especially of those slum players !

Pretentiousness and " showing off " should never be spared. There are few things more anti-educational and more sickening than a performance by youngsters who have been taught to show the audience how sweet and clever they can be, and if they all have the same fault the whole blame rests upon the producer. Training by imitation is another serious though less offensive error. Some young players can be drilled into a mechanically efficient performance imitated from the producer's intonations and movements, much more easily than they can be taught to act, but obviously such a performance can have little value by any standard and is harmful to the players. It might be said that the younger the players the greater is the harm done by this method, and the easier it is to do. On the other hand, special credit is due to any production that preserves, yet shapes to artistic purpose, the spontaneity and freedom from self-consciousness which young players can so delightfully bring to the stage.

These two points raise the embarrassing question of how far the producer is to be criticized overtly. His responsibility for the quality of the performance is often greater than with adults, because young players are more dependent and obedient —and more loyal. To criticize the production publicly may weaken their loyalty and undermine his leadership in other activities besides drama, which the adjudicator can very rarely wish to do even if the production is completely and hopelessly wrong. A few minutes' private talk with the producer may solve this problem very satisfactorily; and, in any case, severe criticism should nearly always be given privately, if necessary, in writing.

To sum up, then, the adjudicator's attitude is as important as his technical qualifications, and should never be Olympian. He must make human allowances, and can rarely judge by standards as purely artistic as those applicable to mature players, though he must make the need for improvement perfectly clear. Perhaps the ideal adjudication is one which leaves players and producer with the feeling that they have done something worth while, that they have a great deal more to do, and that—following the adjudicator's pointers—they are jolly well going to do it.

APPENDIX V

PRODUCING THE PROGRAMME

By John Hampden, M.A.

When so many things have to be done at once, often by a harassed producer working single-handed, it is natural that the programme should often be left at the mercy of the local printer, with results which are sometimes gratifying and sometimes very much the reverse. But the programme is well worth a little care. For one thing, it is studied intently by nearly everybody in the audience before the curtain rises, and so definitely helps to create an atmosphere favourable or unfavourable to the production ; for another, it is broadcast widely afterwards, and is apt to be kept for years by the players and their friends. Finally, like everything else connected with a school production, it has some educative influence. So it is of special importance that the school programme should be a thing of some dignity and beauty—not a monument of bad taste compounded of cheap pink paper and half a dozen ugly, ill-assorted founts of type.

In typography, as in architecture and in many other things, the beautiful is rarely more expensive than the ugly, and is quite often cheaper. For instance, it never costs more—and may cost a little less—to use one or two styles of type than to use six or eight, and the result is usually better beyond comparison.

Founts to avoid as a general rule are condensed types, in which the letters are narrow in proportion to height and usually heavy ; modern faces, in which there is considerable variation in the thickness of different parts of the letter ; and " fancy " types, except when they are very good of themselves and are used with moderation and discretion. Ornaments and heavy frames should also be avoided. On the other hand, a programme plainly set in one fount only, and that a good " old style," such as Aldine Bembo, Caslon, or Garamond, can hardly fail to be an attractive and satisfying piece of work if the paper chosen is a good one with a fairly rough surface. The papers to avoid are calendered and coated " art " ; a good choice as a general rule is a pale cream imitation hand-made.

It is wise to give some general instructions on the above lines, even when dealing with printers of high standing, who can be trusted to produce a dignified programme and can be left very much to themselves. If such a firm is not available, or is too expensive, it is usually good policy to avoid firms of moderate size, such as those which print small provincial papers, and go to a jobbing printer working on a smaller scale. As a rule his prices are low, and he is anxious to please and willing to discuss problems, and sometimes he will become really enthusiastic. If he does not possess the required founts he can get the programme set for a small extra charge by a firm which caters for jobbing printers. He should always be allowed to add his imprint in small type on the back or the last page.

In any case, printers should be approached well in advance with a draft of the programme, so that preliminary arrangements can be made and estimates secured. " Copy " should be set out quite plainly with much the same details as in a professional programme, and the players' initials and names (not names and initials) given as though they were adults. If the characters are set down in order of appearance on the stage this helps the audience, and avoids any question of precedence. A cover design by a member of the school is an attractive addition, and involves no cost beyond the making of a line block. The " copy " should be sent to the printer a fortnight or more in advance, the proofs should not be passed for press until the last possible moment as a precaution against unexpected changes in the cast, and the type should be kept standing until the last performance in case a further supply of programmes is required.

PRINTED IN GREAT BRITAIN AT
THE PRESS OF THE PUBLISHERS

A LIST OF PLAYS FOR GIRLS AND WOMEN
A LIST OF PLAYS FOR BOYS AND MEN
Compiled by
THE BRITISH DRAMA LEAGUE

Each list contains full details of over 200 plays, classified and indexed.

THE " MODERN PLAYS " SERIES
Edited by JOHN HAMPDEN

Fifteen Modern Plays, 3s. 6d. net. Ten Modern Plays, Nine Modern Plays, Eight Modern Plays for Juniors, Seven Modern Plays for Younger Players, Six Modern Plays for Little Players, each vol. 2s. net (School edition, 1s. 3d.; Six Modern Plays, 1s.). Four Modern Plays, Three Modern Plays and a Mime, each 9d. net. With acting notes on every play. Full prospectuses of these and many other plays post free.

MIMES AND MIMING
by ISABEL CHISMAN *and* GLADYS WILES

A book for beginners as well as those who have already discovered the delights of miming. Fourteen mimes without acting fees are included. Illustrated.

MODERN DRAMA
by J. W. MARRIOTT

An illuminating survey of modern drama in England, Europe, and America, and a guide to all the most interesting plays of to-day and yesterday. Cloth gilt.

THE NELSON PLAYBOOKS
Edited by JOHN HAMPDEN
Strong limp cloth. 36 volumes.

All the old favourites, such as " She Stoops to Conquer," and many modern plays, including " Four New Plays for Women," by Philip Johnson, Harold Brighouse, etc.; " Five Robin Hood Plays," by Ronald Gow, etc., etc. Lists post free.

NELSON: 35–36 Paternoster Row, London, E.C.4.